SECRET CITY
The Second Generation

To Deeuey —
What fun we had, growing
up together in the Secret City!

Best Wishes,

Jollie

To Linda Krattler Prickett
ORHS Class of 1965

Whose courage, determination,
soaring spirit, and abiding love
continue to inspire us all.

Rest in peace, dear friend.

Growing up in this Secret City, Atomic Energy Capital of the World, we are the children of the brave pioneers who built the atomic bomb. We are the second generation, and although we didn't know it at the time, we were special.

I am honored yet humbled to have grown up in this exceptional environment and it is with great pride that I share with you my childhood memories.

These are my stories, told through my eyes only. Some may remember things a little differently, and of course there are many events in Oak Ridge that I did not experience personally, so I will leave those stories for others to tell. My liberal use of the pronoun "we" is not meant to speak for others. It simply refers to my general feeling of having grown up here in one very, very, very large family. The absence of negative stories is not because I intentionally left them out, but rather because I just don't remember any!

Several years ago, seven of us girls, close friends since early childhood, got together for a special weekend reunion. Then in our fifties, Ellen Gardiner Morgan, Sandy Shapiro Guryan, Gage Frye Woods, Linda Krattler Prickett, Anne Ergen DeLozier, Jane Ann Jett Wheeler, and I gathered at the Morgan home in Knoxville. Having arrived from all over the country, we hugged, laughed, cried, and re-connected as if still at a high school slumber party; only this time, we were also sharing pictures of children and grandchildren. Since then, Linda has passed on, having finally lost her long battle with brain cancer, but in spirit she is always with us.

We got together again recently at the Ergen Ranch in Colorado and re-affirmed what we already knew. Caught up in our own special world, we talked non-stop for three

5

full days, never even bothering to turn on the TV! Those bonds we built growing up together in Oak Ridge can never be broken.

Our fathers were metallurgists, nuclear physicists, enrichment technicians, mathematicians, chemists, purchasing agents, engineers, and carriers of briefcases, probably filled with blue-green powder, heading for Los Alamos. As the story of the Secret City unfolds, I see it as a confirmation of life and a tribute to the first generation, who came here to save the world and stayed on to raise us, the second generation, so beautifully.

And so, to Selma and Ted, John and Helen, Don and Marie, Viola and William, Ruthie and Gil, Shelby and Ruth, Tot and Dorie, Kay, Mac, and Martha, among so many others, thank you for bringing us together and raising us as family, still connected after all these years.

I hope all of you, especially the Oak Ridge High School Class of 1965, will enjoy reading these stories as much as I have enjoyed writing them.

From Teen Talk to today, I love you all.

Tollie

The Prophet

Early in the 1900's a strange 50-year old farmer by the
name of John Hendrix lived in Bear Creek Valley beneath
the foothills in rural East Tennessee. Alone and lost after
the tragic death of his young daughter and the subsequent
departure of his wife and remaining family, he became a
wanderer. As the story goes, he spent forty sleepless nights
alone in the deep forest. When he emerged, filled with
wild thoughts and visions, he began urgently telling friends,
neighbors, and anyone else who would listen, the details,
which turned out to be eerily accurate. He predicted that
the valley would be filled with great buildings. He heard
the sounds of huge engines digging ditches in the mud and
he saw thousands of people scurrying about, creating great
noise and confusion. He said it would help towards
winning "the greatest war that ever will be." "The earth
will shake," he said; "I have seen it. It is coming." People
wondered if his peculiar predictions were the ramblings of
a madman or the true visions of a prophet. Whatever they
thought, various members of the community put pen to
paper and recorded his stories. John Hendrix died in 1915.
Twenty-eight years later, his story was remembered by
relatives and neighbors. Notes were compared, and it
seems that he did indeed tell us of the secret before the
secret ever came to be. John Hendrix is buried atop a hill
in the Hendrix Creek subdivision, here in the Secret City.

Gates and Guards

And so they came, the 75,000. Early in 1942, General
Leslie R. Groves stood on a hill at Elza Gate (the Clinton
side of the city) and gazed out across 59,000 acres of

sparsely populated farmlands, surrounded by foothills of the Great Smokey and Cumberland Mountains, in rural East Tennessee. Geographically sound with a temperate climate, sufficient electricity from TVA, railway access, and a vast water supply, the densely wooded perimeter could be armed and guarded. Secrecy would prevail. He gave the order and the project, code name Manhattan, began. Workers, hired to work on a project they knew little about, soon began to arrive on site. Uprooted and imported, they were exceptional patriots, men and women highly trained in their fields, sworn to secrecy and U.S. Security-cleared. Their mission was to enrich uranium and ultimately build the Atomic Bomb.

The government's official explanation, given to curious neighboring towns in reference to the area's strange goings-on, was that they were building a post-war retirement community for military officers and high-ranking government personnel. The Alexander Inn in Jackson Square was headquarters for all dignitaries, secretly visiting the city. Clandestine meetings and top-secret strategy sessions were held within its walls. When this ruse was developed, little did they know that the historically significant Alexander Inn was destined to become a retirement center, providing for some of these same early workers, some 70 years later. Living here in the Secret City, we proudly consider ourselves the original "gated community".

AEC

When World War II ended in 1945, The Atomic Energy Commission was established to continue developing nuclear technology. Thousands left, but as the Cold War grew colder, many more came to safeguard, protect, defend, and expand this secret community as it evolved into the Atomic City Capital of the World. Once it became clear that" Ghost Town" was not in Oak Ridge's future, work began to insure its success. In 1950, Union Carbide began enriching lithium and once again workers were recruited to build the hydrogen bomb. Oak Ridge soon became the epitome of a government town. Not a military town, but a government town. From the earliest days, we relied immensely on the Atomic Energy Commission and Union Carbide. The people of the United States greatly appreciated the accomplishments and sacrifices which defined that first generation, and we, their children, were the fortunate recipients of that government gratitude. It was not until 1959 that Oak Ridge voted to incorporate, and our own city government gradually took over.

Coming to the Secret City

I was four years old in 1951 when my parents and I moved to Oak Ridge from Cleveland, Tennessee. Daddy took a job working for Union Carbide Nuclear Division at Oak Ridge National Laboratory and later at Y-12, as an estimating engineer. Many of my future friends were already here, living in government-built cemesto houses which by design should already have fallen apart. These "temporary" houses were designated A, B, C, D, E-1, E-2, and F. They were single family units, with A being the smallest, and F the largest. Randomly scattered throughout the city, they were assigned by family size, and only occasionally by employment status. So our unique neighborhoods were intermingled with families of nuclear physicists, security guards, administrators, educators, uranium technicians, cafeteria workers, and so forth.

Our first home was an E-2 apartment at 111 West Farragut Road. It was a four-family unit consisting of two 2-story, 2-bedroom apartments in the center and a small single apartment on each end. Ours had two bedrooms and a bath upstairs, and a living room and kitchen below. Hardwood floors and a fireplace were the only amenities. There was heat, but no air conditioning. We just left the windows and screen doors open all summer.

The West Farragut Road neighborhood was designed so that the back entrances of several homes and apartment buildings faced each other, looking out onto a big open field. Except for the greenbelt areas, all the trees had been cleared by the government back in the original Muddy Boot Days, leaving only spotty grass in most areas. Individuals were beginning to plant shrubs and flowers, and their beautification efforts were generally very rewarding. The land was fertile, as it had been used for farming in years gone by.

Neighbors with names like Papke, Fergerson, Rosser, Kackenmaster, Trivet, Ruckart and Wilhelm quickly became our extended family. On hot summer nights, the adults would sit outside and watch us play, sipping sweet tea in the moonlight until temperatures cooled down enough for sleeping. Well, maybe it wasn't always tea, but we kids didn't know!

Our dads would usually carpool to work because each family was assigned only one on-street parking space and besides, hardly anyone had two cars back then. The town was designed so that each neighborhood had its own school and small shopping center within walking distance. Our district was Elm Grove and we were also close to Townsite (now Jackson Square), which served as the city center and housed a drugstore, movie theater, laundry, post office, and other essential services.

Drippy Popsicles

I remember riding on my daddy's shoulders across the west side of Farragut through a path in the woods, ending at Georgia Avenue where the Theta parking lot is now, on our way to Service Drug Store or the Ridge movie theater. Service Drug Store is now Big Ed's Pizza, and many of its original features still exist. Daddy would buy me a Popsicle (two sticks, please) for the trip home, and I can still see that cherry syrup trickling down my chin onto the back of his neck. When we got back to the apartment, we would get out the hose to wash off my sticky fingers and Daddy's neck. When he turned on the sprinkler, at least a dozen children would suddenly appear, giggling and "running through the hose." Roots were taking hold in the hot summer sun, and this secret city, predicted to disappear, was beginning to thrive.

Carbide

During the 1950's Union Carbide Corporation, the federal government, and the Atomic Energy Commission provided lots of activities, designed to entertain Oak Ridge children and their families.

At Easter there was a huge egg hunt on the green rolling hills of the Atomic Energy Commission building. Otherwise known as "The Castle on the Hill," it is still located just across the Oak Ridge Turnpike from Jackson

Square. We are not talking about cheap plastic eggs. There were real eggs, sugared eggs, giant chocolate bunnies, confections of all kinds and elegant, elaborate prize eggs. Hundreds of parents and children, dressed in Easter bonnets and all the associated finery, would come together to celebrate and fill their baskets. To me it was magical, like a real life version of the board game Candyland. Today I can still picture it, driving down the Turnpike as the grass greens up in the spring.

As the holidays approached, the annual Carbide Christmas Party was an equally enchanting event. Provided for children of all Carbide employees, it was a Saturday afternoon extravaganza, with candy-filled stockings and gifts for everyone, followed by a holiday movie and of course a visit from Santa and the elves.

The Tennessee Valley Authority (TVA) built Melton Hill Dam in 1953. Our Clinch River basin was flooded, and became Melton Hill Lake. Union Carbide built Carbide Park (now Clark Center Park) along its shores. Always open and free of charge, the park was a community playground, providing fishing, swimming, picnic facilities, sports of all kinds, nature trails, and boating for employees and all Oak Ridge citizens. Federal aid was abundant and benefits were plentiful. My brother even named our puppy "Carbide"!

Playground Circus

The city provided outdoor summer programs for children of all ages, one at each elementary school playground. Open all day, five days a week, we were supervised by adults and teenagers. All students were welcome, free of charge. The grand finale at summer's end was the Playground Circus.

Held at the city softball field (now Carl Yearwood Field), it began with a parade. Each playgroup would march in, all decked out in their homemade costumes, playing their hand-made drums and assorted "musical" instruments. The parade was followed by songs, skits, contests, and various shows of talent.

Prizes and awards were presented and my friend and Swank-ette sister, Yolanda Hull, won the title, "Miss Freckles." It seemed like the whole town turned out to cheer for us, and to support and compliment the city's recreation department. I suppose such events in other places would have cousins and grandparents filling the bleachers and cheering us on, but it was different here. Most of our families had arrived alone, from various places around the country, leaving their relatives behind. So we learned at an early age that "family" goes way beyond blood, and that the phrase, "not from 'round here" applied to almost everyone in Oak Ridge

My favorite playground memory is the year we were American Indians. It was either kindergarten or first grade, at Elm Grove School. Most everyone was barefoot for the event, but I got to wear my authentic Cherokee beaded leather moccasins, proudly purchased in a Gatlinburg gift shop on a family trip to the Smokey Mountains. They were extra special because they helped me learn my left foot from my right. The left shoe was missing a few red beads, a clear signal when needed.

We learned to march together in step by reciting in unison this catchy familiar jingle.

> Left, left, left my wife and 49 kids in a starving
> Condition with nothing but gingerbread.
> Think I did right? Right!

Right, by my country, by jingles, I had a good job
when I left, left.
Left my wife…

I always knew which foot to start with. All I had to do was
look down!

We chose our Indian names, made our own feather
headgear and painted our faces. We crafted drums from
oatmeal boxes and string. Some boys had toy bows and
arrows (with strict orders that arrows were to remain in
quivers at all times). We were proud Indian braves and
princesses. I don't remember if anyone "won" or got a
prize. It didn't matter. We were learning team spirit and
how good it felt to be creative and entertain our town.

Howdy, Pahdnuh!

One summer the rodeo came to town. Set up at the softball
field around sundown, it probably wasn't a very big rodeo,
but it WAS a big event. Oak Ridge didn't get many of
these travelling shows because we were still a government
town and acquiring a permit with security clearance was
complicated.

All dressed up in my fancy black and white cowgirl boots ,
corduroy skirt, embroidered vest and red felt hat, complete
with chin strap, I WAS Dale Evans. Even my stick horse,
"Whirly Girl" came along. She soon got in the way, so
Daddy kindly returned her to the corral (our green station
wagon parked in the parking lot). "Howdy, Pahdnuh" and,
"Hello, Little Lady" were common greetings and that was
okay, back then. Pearl-handled six-shooters (cap guns

probably) hung around my hips in fake leather holsters and I was ready for any challenge to "draw" or "twirl". I learned to "whinny" and according to my parents, whinnying and other rodeo talk replaced most of my words for many days afterward. It was cute, they said, but annoying.

There was a carnival atmosphere at the rodeo and souvenir vendors were abundant. My favorites were the "authentic" cowboy lariats. Made of mostly paper and string, they "buzzed" as you twirled them in circles above your head. These lassoes were everywhere, like June bugs on strings, and their sounds rivaled and probably encouraged the katydids on that hot summer night. Cute, they said, but also annoying.

Food Fight

Spring came early one year on Farragut Road, and neighbors decided to share a garden. There was plenty of space in the common field between apartments and more than enough hands to tend the crops. By the end of August the harvest was prolific. Corn had tasseled and huge cucumbers were creeping along the ground. Produce was taking over and there was more than enough to go around. Perfect fodder as inspiration for "The Great Vegetable War," it began late one muggy afternoon. Children gathered. Sides were taken. Then it began. Sticks and giant zucchini became ball bats. Tomatoes and peppers were the balls. Corn stalks became spears and rotten purple eggplants were flying through the air. Onions, squash, okra, beans – nothing was safe! I was removed early, being told, "The big kids are out of control!" When they finally began to attack the melons and pumpkins, enough was enough. Parents reeled them in, hosed them off, and clean-up began. Little did we know back then that here in the Secret City, we may have just witnessed the very first Great American Food Fight!

The Rabid Fox

In July 1953, a rabid fox was spotted roaming around our neighborhood. Doors were locked and no one went outside, especially children. I remember looking out our back door and seeing it walking along the sidewalk which bordered our side of Farragut Road. It was scary.

Our country was at war in Korea during this time and Oak Ridgers were playing a large part in supporting the war effort. Details were known only to those who were actively engaged in working at the nuclear facilities. We understood clandestine operations here in the Secret City. Curiosity was natural, but our heritage was honorable and we trusted the nuclear integrity of those involved. I knew my dad was working on something important, I knew he had our best interests at heart, I knew he loved America, and I knew he was an honest man. There were no more questions left to be answered in the mind of this six-year-old girl.

Without the technology available today, newspapers were very important to everyone. They connected us with what was happening in the world around us. Along with spotty news on radio and television, The Oak Ridger newspaper was our primary and sometimes only source of information. These papers were usually hand-delivered by our local paperboy. A big truck would drop off large bundles of papers tied up with twine, along the sidewalk. The delivery boy would then roll up each one, fill his canvas side sack and distribute the papers to porches throughout the neighborhood. It just so happened that this very same sidewalk was the one chosen as a path by the foaming-at-the-mouth rabid fox.

This time when the big truck delivered the newspapers, the driver stopped and honked his horn repeatedly before moving on. It was the big news we had hoped for. The headlines read, "KOREAN WAR ENDS!" Heads peeked out of kitchen doors and the good news began to spread. Protecting the young paperboy, brave neighbors stood guard, looking out for the fox, while others rushed to grab and help deliver the papers. It was such important news to us because it meant that the Atomic City would not have to build another bomb. Hearts were lightened and celebrations began.
Animal control soon captured the fox and determined that it was indeed rabid. The all-clear signal was given but I was reluctant to play outside for a while. "What about babies with rabies?" I wondered.

Doctors Pray

On August 20, 1953, my brother was born. Grandmother drove up from Cleveland to help out and when the long-awaited event arrived, I was ecstatic! The thought of being a big sister and introducing the new baby to all my neighborhood family was almost more than I could bear.

Now, as the story goes, Dr. William (Bill) Pugh, highly regarded obstetrician who delivered most Oak Ridge babies for many, many years, arrived at the hospital in his pajamas. He slept that night in mother's hospital room, determined to ensure that all was well. During this process, they say, he actually fired two nurses. They probably didn't stay fired for very long, but Dr. Pugh was very serious about birthing babies.

Children were not allowed in the maternity ward at Methodist Hospital, but one of my proudest memories is when my daddy took me to the grassy yard beside the hospital. We had to wait while my grandmother went in to visit. Soon Daddy told me to look way, way up to the top of the building. There in the window was his nurse, holding up my baby brother for me to see. It truly felt like he was waving back at me. Welcome to the world, Robert McCutchen Moore!

Another important doctor at Oak Ridge Methodist Hospital was Dr. Paul Spray. He came to Oak Ridge with his family in 1950 when our hospital was still a small Army facility, and his son Tommy was in my class. My grandmother told us later that she was so impressed with our special hospital. While she was there waiting for Cutch to be born, every so often, someone would come on the loud speaker and say, "Doctors, pray. Doctors, all pray." It really appealed to her spiritual side. What they were really saying was, "Doctor Spray. Doctor Paul Spray." Nobody ever bothered to tell her the difference. After all, it really was a special place indeed.

Cindy

Our family attended church on Tennessee Avenue at Kern Memorial Methodist. Bible School was held five mornings a week for two weeks in the summer. My cousin Cindy Stuart (the closest I have to a sister) would come up from

Cleveland to stay for at least a week. When it was Daddy's turn to drive his carpool, we would walk the half mile from home to church. We followed the Tennessee Avenue sidewalk and it took us directly past Elm Grove School. The summer playground program was in full swing and it was such a temptation to stop and play along the way. What a dilemma! Mommy soon came up with the perfect solution. She would bring along a sack lunch so we could leave Bible School, picnic with her and Baby Cutch, and then stay on for the afternoon session at Elm Grove. She didn't mind, she said, because Cindy and I could help her give Cutch his mid-day bottle. We felt so important. Carefree summer days were a big part of growing up in the Secret City in the 1950's.

Engineering Ingenuity

Haynes Patterson and his parents lived across the street from us in a D house on Farragut Road. Big trees in the woods reached nearly up to his back door. His dad built a tree house for him, complete with electricity and phone lines. It was so ahead of the times, a clear example of engineering ingenuity. Like a miniature house in a tree, it was very futuristic.

We did occasionally have property line disputes as children. I remember hearing," This is my properly"; "No it is not, this is my properly"; " Is not, it's the government's property." End of discussion. It was never an issue at Hanes's tree house. We were always welcome, as long as the GIRLS KEEP OUT sign was not posted.

Doris and Frank Binford and daughter Mandy lived next door to the Pattersons. Mandy was my best friend. They

19

were the first family in the neighborhood to own a color television set. Of course we children were enthralled with it but it fostered some rather heated discussions among the adults. Questions such as, "Do we watch it with the lights on or off?", "Do we have to pull the drapes in the daytime?", "How close to the set should we sit?", "Will the volume hurt our ears?", "Is it safe for young children?", and "Does it give off radioactivity?" were hot topics and our neighborhood Secret City Scientists were determined to come up with the right answers. I'm not sure they ever reached a consensus, and as I recall, the light switch was flicked off and back on again for quite some time. There was no such thing as remote control so there was a lot of physical activity associated with watching television. The volume control knob was constantly in need of re-adjusting, depending upon who was watching, and the rabbit-ears antenna on top of the set was always being bumped and re-aligned. There were no "couch potatoes" in those days!

Childhood Secrets

I had a personal experience with secret-telling at a very young age. When I was six years old, I asked my friend Mandy what it meant that she was adopted. Most likely I had overheard an adult conversation and I was curious. Mandy didn't know she was adopted, and I had inadvertently told a secret. Mandy learned something from me that she was not yet supposed to know. I felt horrible. Her dear Aunt Olive was visiting from Pennsylvania and she came over to our house to give me a hug and reassure me that they all understood what had happened. Our families remained close throughout the years, but thinking back, I still feel responsible. There were unintended consequences, which are often the results when secrets are revealed.

Halloween

Halloween was fun on Farragut Road. We wore homemade costumes because there was no Wal-Mart and ready-mades were just not available. We begged our parents not to make us wear coats to cover up our disguises, convinced the neighbors would never guess who we really were. Sheets with holes cut out for eyes, raggedy clothes with bandanna-tied parcels on long sticks, Lone Ranger masks, long black robes and broomsticks made their way along the street as soon as the sun went down. Neighbors played along, "puzzled" as to our identity as they served up punch and popcorn balls, caramel apples and handfuls of candy.

When I was seven, Cutch was too young to go trick-or-treating so I, dressed as a Hollywood glamour gal, carried two treat bags, one for each of us. With Mommy's sable fur draped around my neck, I wore her fancy beaded dress and smart black pillbox hat with polka-dotted veil. Bright red lipstick, pearls, and her red high heels completed the ensemble. Soon the other children were way ahead of me so I ditched the heels along the way. Later that evening Daddy took the flashlight and retrieved the heels, making sure they made their way safely back to Mommy's closet.

Education Expectations

Not many non-military school districts can boast of being built under direct orders of the United States Army; but in

1943 when they summoned Dr. Alden H. Blankenship from his work at Columbia University to assume a top-secret, strange and mysterious assignment as superintendent of schools in the backwoods of East Tennessee, history was about to be made.

Faced with the task of hiring a staff of superior educators, capable of contributing more than just subject matter and charged with the safety and development of their students, he quickly hired exceptional teachers from 36 different states, enough to staff nine elementary schools, a junior high school, and a senior high school. The first graduating class in 1944 included 50 students. When our class graduated in 1965, we were the largest ever, close to 600.

Education was very important to first generation Oak Ridgers. So many of them had earned their doctorates and very high level skills and training. They came here for such a complicated yet specific purpose. Their mission was successful, and expectations for their children were naturally very high.

The Schools

In the beginning, nine neighborhood districts were established within the city. Each one was centered around a school and included a small shopping center within walking distance for those living inside its borders. These districts were Cedar Hill, Elm Grove, Glenwood, Highland View, Linden, Pine Valley, Scarboro, Willow Brook, and Woodland. I attended Elm Grove School, on Tennessee Avenue, for kindergarten through second grade, Glenwood, near East Drive, for third grade through sixth, Jefferson Junior High on Kentucky Avenue for seventh, eighth, and ninth, and then Oak Ridge High School on Providence Road for my sophomore, junior, and senior years.

The Elm Grove Shopping Center included Mr. Blankenship's barber shop, a Piggly Wiggly Grocery Store and McGinley's Elm Grove Drug Store. Our friend Kyle Miller, the butcher, could cut any meat, custom ordered, and he often knew just what his customers preferred, even before they placed an order. The soda fountain at the drugstore was famous for egg cream sodas and the best toasted pimento cheese sandwiches in the universe. The grown-ups liked to go downstairs around holiday time, but why they went still remains a secret to me! Mr. McGinley was partners with Mr. Hoskins from Clinton, and Hoskins Drug Store, located across the street from the Anderson County Courthouse, still serves up some of the best southern-style food you can find in Anderson County.

Beautiful Mrs. Valentine was my kindergarten teacher at Elm Grove School, and I have looked forward to the beginning of school ever since the first day I walked timidly into her classroom. These were the times when school began after Labor Day in the fall, when pleated plaid skirts, cardigan sweaters, knee-high socks and saddle shoes were all the rage, and ended in the spring, when we switched to sun dresses and sandals.

The concept of neighborhood schools made very good sense at the time. They were all built to the same plan, and included grades K-6. They all had spacious, well-equipped playgrounds, cafeterias, music rooms, art rooms, and a full gym with a curtained stage for assemblies and other performances. Each homeroom class had an active volunteer room-mother and every child's birthday was celebrated with treats and favors, followed by extra recess or games in the gym. The entire staff, from the bus drivers to our principal, knew us all by name and the school nurse was there to help us with a skinned knee or the occasional "mommy blues".

There was, however, a more important reason for full staffing and knowing the children so well. It was the possibility of a city-wide evacuation in case of enemy action or perhaps even a nuclear disaster. We wore dog tags, engraved with our names, parents' names and some kind of code telling our evacuation route and where to meet up with our parents outside the gates. There were air raid drills during which we would put our heads on our desks, be silent, and wait for further instructions. We might be told to climb under our desks and wait for the all-clear sirens. Or we might line up and exit the building, walking up to Tennessee Avenue, from Elm Grove, or to East Drive from Glenwood.

At this point, in a real emergency, cars or buses would be waiting to deliver us to undisclosed locations and later re-unite us with our families. Emergency routes from the city went past the guard gates or down G-road. Known today as Key Springs Road, G-road is a densely wooded, fairly obscure, winding road connecting Outer Drive, along the city's north ridge to State Road 61, in the valley below.

This scenario explains further why school staff responsibilities reached far beyond teaching and included security clearance and extensive training. There was no telling how long we might remain their responsibility. I have no memory of being scared during these times, just protected and cared for. Considering the times we lived in, that amazes me still, and is a great tribute to all those who were entrusted with our care.

Old Glory

We grew up with air raid sirens, heard frequently as the equipment was tested on a regular basis. Fire safety was another major concern. Of course it always is, but a fire in our valley could have catastrophic consequences if it were to get out of control. The Japanese had used setting fires as a weapon during the war, so naturally there was concern and the government made sure we were well-prepared and well-equipped to handle an emergency of that nature. Schools had student fire marshals who accompanied the firemen on monthly safety checks. Each homeroom elected a marshal and his or her job was to make sure all doors and windows were closed, the room was secure and all classmates were accounted for during these drills, which occurred frequently and unannounced.

We signed pledges to help ensure fire safety at home, school, and throughout the community. The Fire Chief spoke to us in assembly. He had us raise our right hand and yell, "No fires in my house, NO SIR!" and encouraged us to use that greeting whenever we encountered a fireman around town.

Each class, beginning in kindergarten, elected a member of the Safety Patrol. They wore white cross belts and badges and helped manage traffic procedures and busses both before and after school. Their knowledge and skills were also important because they would help to maintain order in case of an evacuation. The Safety Patrol was in charge of the flag ceremony. Every morning the American Flag was raised and every afternoon it was lowered. Students and adults stopped what they were doing to watch this procedure, which was taken seriously and performed correctly and with honor every time. We learned respect for Old Glory at a very young age.

Bicycle safety was also a primary concern. Every so often the city would hold safety checks in the school parking lots on Saturday mornings. Police officers would check our tires and brakes and drill us on the proper hand signals. If we passed inspection, we could register our bikes, receive stickers, and sign commitment cards. We rode our bicycles all over town, so these were significant regulations.

As we got older, we took long bike hikes, and could even end up at the rock quarry. Located in an area of the nuclear facilities off-limits to the public today, it is a giant hole in the ground, completely filled with water. Created earlier from excavations, history claims that no one could determine how deep it was. How or why the quarry excavation site became filled with water is if not an intentional secret, at least still a mystery to the general public. Peering over the ledge, we wondered if stories of stolen cars, scientific experiments gone wrong, and dead (possibly murdered) bodies were somewhere below us, in the depths of those dark, cold waters. We never got an answer, so it remains an unsolved mystery, here in the Secret City.

Measles and Marshmallows

In the first grade at Elm Grove I missed 167 days of school. I had mumps, measles, chicken pox, scarlet fever, whooping cough, tonsillitis, allergies and asthma, just to name a few. Nevertheless, I made straight A's, thanks to a dedicated school system and a devoted teacher. Mrs. Wilson would sometimes stop by my house to check up on me and deliver homework. She would take time to visit and bring homemade cards and well-wishes from my friends at Elm Grove School. She also brought me paper and art supplies so I could write thank-you notes, which she would later pick up and take back to the children. Once the bus driver stopped and honked the horn so Mommy would come out and tell everyone how I was doing.

Mr. Hartley J. Schultz was our principal and Mrs. Ella Evenson taught second grade. Having been recruited from Pelican Rapids, Minnesota, her unique accent was both charming and intriguing to us. She told us stories of growing up in Crystal-Lida Beaches and it seemed like a magical storyland. Grandmotherly and soft, she was affectionate, and hugging her was like hugging a marshmallow. It was extraordinary, this sense of family we shared.

Doctor Preston

Dr. Lewis Preston was my hero. My parents said it seemed like I spent half of my early life in his office. He was important to me because not only did he prescribe medicines but his smile and good nature went a long way towards making me feel better. Sometimes my mother had to sit up with me all night. We would try to sleep, sitting in bed propped up, back to back, because whenever I would slip down, my hard coughing would keep us from sleeping at all. He provided wonderful support and helpful advice to the families of his sick young patients. Sometimes Dr. Preston would actually sit with me on the floor of his office and build toy airplanes out of tongue depressors. Special memories of a very special man. Dr. Preston helped take care of Oak Ridge children for many years. Even though he was a pediatrician, I could still get in to see him, even after I was off to college. Many years later, when our children were growing up, Dr. Preston always had a safe, up-to-date vehicle, and could often be seen, driving up and down the icy hills of Oak Ridge and everyone knew he was on his way to a sick child who could not get to him. His legacy cannot be measured.

ABC Order

All the original streets in Oak Ridge were arranged in alphabetical order. Tennessee Avenue runs parallel to the Oak Ridge Turnpike, and roughly parallel to Outer Drive. The roads connecting Tennessee and Outer Drive are named for states, running alphabetically from California to Delaware, Florida, Georgia, and so forth. Side streets are alphabetical as well. For example, Cahill Lane is at the bottom of California, Clarion is at the top, and Chatham is half-way up the hill, in-between. That is how we learned our way around town. Even today, as new homes are built, the alphabetical tradition continues, whenever possible. Streets today go from Alabama to Wisconsin, and all points in between. One thing we second generationers have in common is our sense of direction. Most of us don't have one! As we grew up and moved away, we got lost a lot, but we really knew how to alphabetize!

Lot Number One

That same year the Atomic Energy Commission Act was passed by the 84th Congress and Executive Order 10657. The following year, July 11, 1956, the Oak Ridge Community Disposal Declaration was similarly passed, allowing for citizens to purchase their property from the United States Government. This long-awaited event was a milestone in the development of The Secret City.

On January 14, 1957, my parents bought our home. Listed as Lot # 1 on the plat map of the entire city of Oak Ridge, it was .049 acres, conveyed by deed from the United States of America for the sum of $2,900.00. It was still subject to governmental regulations on the use or occupancy of the premises and mortgage payments were $30.77 per month. Owners were to pay to the Atomic Energy Commission an annual charge (amount unknown) as compensation for municipal services provided. I doubt it was very much.

Our house was down at the very end of the lane, which was surrounded on three sides by dense greenbelt. The term "dead end street" was a very strange concept to an eight – year-old girl, and those woods were a little scary to me at first. I once heard someone say that these cemesto houses were only meant to last seven years. They were built in the early 1940's. I was told, "Don't worry, they are not about to collapse anytime soon." I wasn't convinced, so I kept looking for evidence of a little "crumbling", just in case.

Our one designated parking space was uphill from the house. From the street, there were 16 concrete steps downhill, a short sidewalk, and nine wooden steps back up to the front porch. Oak Ridge houses were built without driveways and garages. In our case, no matter how hard they might try, all the brilliant scientists at the lab could not have figured out how to add them; but to us it was a minor inconvenience. My parents never complained about carrying groceries up and down. Steps were good exercise, they said. You see, we loved Oak Ridge much more than we loved convenience. We had two bedrooms, a furnace room (no longer used for coal delivery), a living room, kitchen, one small bathroom, and a large front porch. Electric baseboard heaters, hardwood floors, a fireplace and a large picture window were the "amenities". Still we had no air conditioning but our high elevation and shade trees overhead kept us fairly cool and it was nice to sleep with the windows open.

Kinstry

Not long after we moved to Chatham Lane, the McKinstrys moved in next door. Their daughter Linda was my age and son Doug was just a year or so older than Cutch. We hit it off right away and it didn't take long for our families to become close friends, forming a solid bond that has remained unbroken through all these years. Linda and I were inseparable in those days. Our bedroom windows faced each other across the yard and together we rode the bus to Glenwood every day. Linda and Doug's mother Kay died when we were very young. It was painful and very sad for a long time, until Mom and Dad introduced us all to Martha Parks from Cleveland. Martha was our saving grace. She and Mr. McKinstry fell in love and married, and "Martita" has been the loving strength of their family ever since. It really is an Oak Ridge thing, these extended families.

Linda and I loved to eavesdrop on the adults, especially late on weekend nights. Often sleeping over at one house or the other, we would talk and giggle 'til the wee hours, then sleep 'til noon the next day. We heard jokes and stories, but we didn't always quite catch on. For example, once the McKinstrys' house was being re-painted. One of the painters fell off the ladder, jumped up and hollered, "Oh, purple onions!!!" We had no clue why, but the term "purple onions" always brought laughter to Chatham Lane, so we just laughed right along with everyone else.

The Ledbetters were our neighbors on the left side, at 106 Chatham. Their two daughters, Cynthia and Nancy, quickly became good friends with Kinstry and me. On warm summer mornings, we girls would spread out large hand-made quilts in their back yard, in the soft grass at the edge of the thick woods. We set up all our dolls and teddy bears around the edges, and prepared for a picnic. Dogs and boys were NOT welcome. We had cute little wicker strollers and doll buggies and a variety of mostly homemade outfits for our dolls and various stuffed animals. We often went for strolls together, up and down the lane, showing off our miniature families and all their fancy adornments.

When it was time for lunch, Mrs. Ledbetter would provide us with a large jar of peanut butter and a bottle of maple syrup, which we mixed together in a big green bowl with a wooden spoon. We then spread this creamy sweet concoction onto thick slices of soft white bread. We finished off our picnic with a thermos of ice cold milk and a large bag of potato chips. Boys and dogs were still not welcome. They did, however, try to sneak up on us from time to time, in an attempt to kidnap or at least disturb our dolls. Most of their attempts were unsuccessful because we became very good at chasing them off with loud, high-pitched voices, heard clearly, all the way up to California Avenue.

Mr. William Lawrence McKinstry, affectionately known as "Mac", soon earned the title "Mayor of Chatham Lane." He always seemed to know what was happening in the neighborhood. Linda cleverly changed the name of our street to "Chatter Lane", a much more appropriate title. Since there were so many Lindas in our class, she became well- known as Kinstry, and that's what we girls call her, still today. My dad's Chatham Lane title was "Doctor Moore". He had friends in Medical out at the Lab, and would provide as needed, whether it was co-pyronil for Mother's allergies or Epsom salts for aching feet. The Mayor and Doctor Moore shared many good times together through the years.

Sooooo-eeeeee!

Saturday afternoon TV ballgames often led to late nights in our living room. Mac was a huge fan of the Arkansas Razorbacks. He was born and raised in Arkansas, and the governor bestowed upon him the coveted title, "Arkansas Traveler". I can still hear him stammer out, "Now l-l-l-let me tell you 'bout the Hogs!" His "sooooo-eeeees" were second to none. Mayor Mac played saxophone and clarinet with the legendary Artie Shaw in the 1940's, and they all loved listening to Mom's 78 rpm records, singing and dancing to the music of the Big Bands. When they finally played (or sang) "Good Night, Ladies" or "Three O'clock in the Morning," Martha would say firmly, "Lawrence, it's time to go home." So down the porch steps they went, and across the yard, singing, "Show me the way to go home.

I'm tired and I want to go to bed..." Good times on
Chatter Lane!

Woodland Secrets

There was a small creek hidden deep in the woods beyond
the end of Chatham Lane. We could swing across it on
vines or balance on broken down trees. The boys would
find frogs and salamanders, and it was especially fun after a
big rain. Up the hill and deep in the woods behind our
house we discovered an old abandoned softball field,
complete with a rusty broken down backstop. We were
intrigued by thoughts of pre-war children playing there,
then maybe being forced to give it up. I wondered how
they felt and what had become of them. We children kept
our discovery secret for a very long time. We also found
patches of daffodils, lilies, and iris, and flat-stone
pathways, going nowhere, most likely remnants of
farmhouses long ago. We even discovered a path leading
from our house through the woods all the way up to Outer
Drive. What was it used for, we wondered, and by whom?

30 Statues

There are 12 houses on Chatham Lane, and at one time
there were 34 children in the neighborhood. Kick-the-Can,
Hide and Seek, bicycles, tricycles, roller skates, and a giant
snail hopscotch were such fun. We loved to stay out after
dark when the streetlights came on. Families called us
home by distinct bells and whistles. They could probably
be heard a mile away, or at least up to California and down
into the woods. My daddy would whistle, "whee-oo-

wheet". Another imitated a Bob-white, and another rang a cowbell; all were easily recognized and identified by anyone on the lane.

We children loved to go on neighborhood scavenger hunts. One of the parents would give us a basket and a long list of strange and unusual items and we were to collect every object on the list. Off we went to search the area, knocking on doors and combing the woods until every single item was located. Sometimes it took all day! When the task was finally completed, there would be treats of some sort to reward us for all of our hard work. Looking back, I see now that this game served as a great baby-sitter, giving our mothers a few well-deserved personal hours!

When we were older, we still had scavenger hunt parties, only then each guest would be given a copy of the same list and a grand prize would be given to the first one back with a completed collection of objects. We even played after we began driving, when the items on the lists became a lot more difficult to obtain. Scavenger hunts for older teenagers were a lot more challenging and also a lot more fun!

One night we stayed out after dark playing hide-and-seek. It began to get late, and we could not find Steve Elbert. Certain he was cleverly hiding somewhere in the woods, we searched and searched and began calling his name. Pretty soon the whole neighborhood joined in the search. After what seemed like hours, his parents found him. Sound asleep in his bed, he had forgotten to tell anyone he was going home! We also played "King on the Mountain," "Freeze Tag," Kick Ball", "Mother May I", "Red Light, Green Light," and "Swing the Statue." Mom told me that sometimes they would look up the lane and see 30 child-size statues, frozen in time, just like the New Orleans street mimes in that other Jackson Square.

Ancestors

As we grew up in Oak Ridge, prestige and respect had little to do with where we lived. I was never aware of expectations or definitions based on family heritage, work status, culture, or ethnic origins. Everyone was from somewhere else and ancestry is something I never really thought about. On the other hand, when we went to visit relatives in Cleveland, it was a different feeling all together. The Hardwicks, on my mother's side, were founders of the city, having arrived there in the 1800's. My great grandfather Moore, on my dad's side, was once the sheriff of Bradley County. It seemed that wherever we went or whatever we did, people were either related to us or were friends with us or knew our relatives. It was different here, and in a lot of ways, it was better.

Our neighborhood school districts were our world, and boundaries were based on where we lived, not who we were. We were trail blazers, free to choose our own paths without any pre-conceived limits or expectations. The important thing is that families, whether formed by blood, by love, or simply by sharing a common bond, played a huge part in forming the lives we shared as both first and second generation Oak Ridgers. Now we become ancestors to the future generations of our Secret City and continuing to share this strong heritage will surely serve them well.

Asking Inky

As the Secret City grew stronger, it was time to gradually cut our government ties and take over our own government. There was talk of incorporating, and the Oak Ridger newspaper began printing a column entitled "Ask Inky". Through this media, citizens asked and answered questions about what to expect, how it would affect us, would we be successful financially, and what form of government should we choose, etc. Once it was all figured out, with the help and full support of the federal government, the City of Oak Ridge incorporated in 1959. We elected our first mayor, Mr. Al Bissell, who led us wisely down a winding path and his legacy is immeasurable. Heartfelt thanks to his family, especially his daughter Elaine, my good friend and Swank-ette Sister, for sharing him with us during all those years.

We didn't ask what our parents did at work. We had a vague idea, but details were not to be known. There was no "Bring Your Child to Work Day." Rather, it was "Don't tell your child what you did at work today." Everyone knew the timely and now well-known phrase associated with our Secret City:

> What you see here,
> What you do here,
> When you leave here,
> Let it stay here.

Another friend and Swank-ette Sister, Sally Sapirie, was loved and respected by her classmates, and her father, Samuel R. Sapirie, was loved and respected by the city of Oak Ridge. Their family came to the Secret City in 1946, when Sally was less than a year old. Then in 1951, Mr. Sapirie took over as head of the Atomic Energy

Commission's Oak Ridge Office, which he continued to manage successfully for 21 years. We were always welcome in their D house up on Ogden Circle.

My dad was a project estimator. He took great pride in the fact that during all those years, in spite of expenditures of more than 11 billion dollars, there was never any official accusation or investigation related to fraud, misappropriation, or misuse of government funds. It was due, he said, to the character, intelligence, and integrity of Sam Sapirie. Thank you, Mr. and Mrs. Sapirie, for being there for us during all those years.

Workplace safety was of paramount importance to those who were in charge of Oak Ridge, and their responsibility included every inch of the entire government facility, city included. Large billboards displayed around town proudly kept track of how many days had gone by since an accident had occurred. Bonuses, safety awards, and the Carbide Savings Plan were merit-based and abundant, and they benefitted everyone in the Secret City.

By 1960, Oak Ridge was still listed on very few maps and that same year the official Guide to Tennessee made no mention of our existence. It was years later before the words Oak Ridge appeared on an Interstate sign. Today our award-winning Secret City Festival brings in people from all over the world, and we appear proudly on every map and GPS system available.

Glenwood School

I have sketchy yet clear impressions of Glenwood School. When Mrs. Blakely had a mental breakdown, Mrs. Amick replaced her as our third grade teacher. Understanding our confusion and concern, she soothed us with music and culture from other lands. She brought her record player into the classroom and enchanted us with beautiful authentic recordings. She taught us to sing magical songs like "Funiculi, Funicula!", "The Campbells are Coming", "Allouette", "Chinese Legend of the Blue Willow", "My Bonnie Lies Over the Ocean", and "An English Country Garden".

She also had a funny side. The door to the faculty lounge was painted bright green, and it was always closed. The popular song, "Green Door", by Jim Lowe was currently playing on the radio and Mrs. Amick taught us the words. One afternoon we sneaked down the hall and gathered outside the door for our "Serenade to the Staff":

> Midnight, one more night without sleepin'
> Watchin', til the children (our version) come creepin'
> Green Door, what's that secret you're keepin'?
> GREEN DOOR!

The door flew open, the faculty laughed, and we finally got to peek inside. That mysterious green door was not so secret anymore.

Mrs. Smithson was my teacher in both fourth and fifth grades. In her split-grade classes we traveled with the explorers, learned geography, current events, and lots of math. Each year in addition to homeroom we also had music, art, gym, special projects, and of course recess. Cafeteria food was really good. Parents and others were frequent guests around our lunch tables. Home-cooked meals, chess pie and pineapple upside down cake were the norm. Many members of the original cafeteria staff were still here and we benefitted from their recipes, saved from early dormitory life, feeding the 75,000 first generationers.

We participated a lot in weekly assemblies, which were re-created for our families in the evening. In third grade the school prepared a rather elaborate Christmas program. Kinstry played a solo on the steel guitar and our class performed the carol, "O Holy Night". Jane Ann's beautiful voice "nailed it" during the school assembly and that night, when it was my turn to solo, I screeched. Never mind that the music teacher apologized for pitching it too high. My singing career was short-lived and over. Future solos were never more than the spoken word!

I wasn't much of an athlete, but I loved the playground at Glenwood School. There were less rules and regulations than we have today, so we could pile as many kids as possible on the merry-go-round and then make it go as fast as the "pushers" could run. There were monkey bars, slides, see-saws, jungle gyms and whirl-arounds, all made by the U.S. government of solid steel, sturdy and strong. Big metal swing sets lined the top of the hill by the woods. We could swing as high as possible and jump out, even if we skinned a knee. We played "girls chase the boys" and "boys chase the girls. "Red Rover", "Blind Man's Bluff", and "Drop the Hankie" were some of the organized games. Hopscotch and jump rope down by the sixth grade entrance seemed to go on for hours. Naturally recess was everyone's favorite time of the day!

Polio

Polio was a big concern during these years. I remember lining up with children from all over the city in the Elm

39

Grove parking lot to receive the Salk vaccine. Oak Ridge scientists were credited with improving these vaccines through the liquid centrifuge process, and being a government town, it was only natural that we were among the first to receive them. We children lined up on the stairs to the left side of the stoop facing Tennessee Avenue. Nurses in white uniforms (probably Red Cross)were waiting at the top, and gave each of us a paper cup (like the small ketchup cups in fast-food restaurants) containing a white sugar cube with a dot of red liquid on it. We ate the cube, and then walked down the steps on the other side, into the waiting arms of our parents, who were still not totally convinced that we were not all going to come down with polio. We of course didn't, but before my brother Cutch was old enough for his vaccine, he was diagnosed with polio. It turned out to be a false alarm, only a rare virus, but that was indeed an uneasy and very scary time.

Brownies

Wednesdays were Brownie Scout days at Glenwood. We were allowed to wear our uniforms to school. My mother volunteered to be the leader, and so troop 30 met every week at my house on Chatham Lane. Daddy said she couldn't carry a tune in a bucket, but boy did she love to sing! After school on Wednesdays, about eight of us girls would pile onto the bus, ready for whatever this week's adventure had to offer. The bus let us off at California Avenue, and we proceeded to march down Chatham Lane. Arms linked, in our sturdy Buster Brown shoes, thin little scalloped brown anklets, brown shirtwaist dresses, and brown beanies perched on top of our heads, down the lane we went, singing our Brownie theme song:

I've got something in my pocket.
It belongs across my face.
I keep it very close at hand,
In a most convenient place.
I bet you couldn't find it
If you guessed a long, long while,
So I'll take it out and put it on.
It's a great big Brownie Smile!

I have no idea what the neighbors were thinking, but at that moment, we ruled the Lane!

Sixth Grade

In sixth grade I really began to love school. I always liked sitting beside my friend Ellen. We wrote notes and shared reports, and ever since those elementary days, she has been my strong, quiet support in everything we do. Mrs. Ardela Worthington was our teacher. A beautiful lady with soft white hair and perfectly manicured red fingernails, she dressed in style, which made us feel important and respected because she took the time to look so special, just for us. She was dedicated to our education. Besides the basics, we wrote poetry, put on a French language play for assembly, and we studied biology. We even dissected a chicken. Not one that she bought at the grocery store, but a live one, whose neck was wrung outside by the classroom door. She taught us a lot about how things were done in the old days, but observing this procedure was optional. I declined!

Mrs. Worthington came to dinner at our house one night. We ate spaghetti and she sold my parents our first set of World Book Encyclopedias. These books are still in our bookcase today, available to our grandchildren, and a reminder of just how important education was to Oak Ridgers, and still is today. The New York Yankees beat the Milwaukee Braves in the World Series and NASA launched Pioneer One. She sometimes let us bring in our transistor radios so we could hear these and other current events as they happened.

Our lives changed drastically when bombs exploded inside Clinton High School.

Clinton High School

On August 27, 1956, the small town of Clinton, just seven miles from Oak Ridge, made headlines around the world. Twelve young black students walked into Clinton High School and became the first in the southeast to desegregate a state-supported school. Oak Ridge schools, being run by the federal government, were integrated on September 6, 1955, just after the historic Supreme Court mandate, Brown vs. Board of Education. Photographed by Life Magazine, 42 black students entered Oak Ridge High School without incident, and with our wide diversity as a city, I was not even aware of these issues at the time.

Two years later, we were in Mrs. Worthington's sixth grade class when white supremacists set off huge devastating bombs inside Clinton High School. We were horrified. Our parents had built a huge bomb to save the world from bad guys. How could this be happening here? We grew up a lot as we began to absorb the true significance of all that was happening around us, and Mrs. Worthington did her best to both educate us and keep us calm.

We were horrified, but we were not helpless. The community rallied 'round, and work began to clean up Linden Elementary School, here in Oak Ridge. It had been abandoned as our population was changing and it was available. Secret City officials quickly offered it to Clinton so that the high school students could continue their education. ORHS students, CSHS students, mothers, neighbors, and staff came with mops, brooms, and paintbrushes. Within four days the school was ready for use.

Our class collected money by doing odd jobs for pennies, and giving up allowances and picture shows. We put the money, ten dollars, in a jar and I, along with Jean Baker, Steve Elbert, Frances Williams, and Lyn Funkhouser, went to the school to give the money to the principal, Mr. Human. He invited us to come back and present our money to the school in an assembly. It wasn't the amount, he said, but the thought behind the gift that mattered. As chairman of the committee, it was my job to make the presentation speech and I had no idea what to say. "Just speak from your heart," Mrs. Worthington told me, and her advice served me well.

Clinton High School students gave us a standing ovation and the Oak Ridger wrote a nice article about our efforts. Pitching in for a common cause was part of our collective soul, even at the young age of eleven.

On opening day, a caravan of 16 buses carried the students from Clinton to their new high school in Oak Ridge. The buses were integrated, and freedom prevailed. It still gives me goose bumps to think about the Oak Ridge High School Band, standing tall in formation at Linden, welcoming their school rivals by playing the Clinton High School Alma Mater.

Spooky

Camp Friendship was centered in a big old rambling farmhouse located near the guard station on the west end of Oak Ridge Turnpike. Deep in the thickly wooded greenbelt, it was one of the few original landmarks the government had left standing inside the city limits. It was spooky, and it was a perfect location for a Girl Scout day camp. In addition to spending a week at a time day-camping in the summer, we occasionally got to have an overnight. We brought pillows and bed-rolls to spread out on the big wrap-around porch. We made sit-upons for around the campfire and cut green sticks for marshmallows. Building safe fires was a major concern, both as scouts and as citizens of the Secret City. As loyal scouts, we knew the Smokey Mountain Anthem by heart:

> Smokey the Bear, Smokey the Bear,
> Growlin' and a-prowlin' and a-sniffin' the air
> He can smell a fire before it starts to flame,
> That's why they call him Smokey
> And that's how he got his name!

Dinner was hobo packs (our version of sloppy Joes) baked in the coals, and of course, s'mores. "S'more's", like, "I want s'more." Not smores, like smurfs. Scouts invented them and it was important to pronounce it right. Otherwise, you are "not from 'round here", and everyone will know.

At bedtime, we lowered the flag in the official Girl Scout ceremony, sang one last song as we carefully put out the campfire, and climbed into our bed rolls. We couldn't sleep, wondering who or what was upstairs (we were not allowed on the second floor) and what was that creeping sound we heard? Then the ghost stories began. First was the famous but not-really-so-scary ghost story, ending with:

    (scary voice)   "It floats... It floats... it floats...
    (whisper)   "Wh-what floats?"
    (loud voice)   "IVORY SOAP!!!)"

This one startled us, but then it made us laugh. Soon someone would tell the famous really scary story of "The Hook". Certain that he was lurking somewhere in the woods, it was scarier to us than a nuclear attack. I thought I would never close my eyes again.

But I did, and we woke up early to a clear green Oak Ridge morning. Gathered at the campfire, listening to the mocking birds, we cooked our breakfast doughboys. We wrapped canned biscuits around green sticks, and toasted them like marshmallows. Then we pulled them off and filled the holes with butter and homemade strawberry jam. Nothing ever tasted any better. Well, maybe Big Ed's Pizza, but that's another story...

Rainy Days and Mysteries

It was an exciting day when Daddy decided to screen in the front porch. A basic project by today's standards, but it was new and creative back then. It was like adding a whole new room onto our small B house. Furnishings included the usual porch furniture, grandmother's wooden rocking chair and metal glider, but we also had a roll-away bed, so we could actually take turns sleeping outside! I loved listening to the crickets and tree frogs and other music of the night. On rainy afternoons I would curl up with a bowl of leftover spaghetti and my latest Nancy Drew Mystery and read for hours.

I had a lot of slumber parties, and sometimes my friends would bring their blankets and pillows and we would sleep out on the porch. Every once in a while, when everyone else was asleep, we would sneak out and go yard-rolling. We added to our stash of hidden toilet paper gradually, so no one would notice an occasional missing roll. The screen door was creaky, but once we learned to paint the hinges with baby oil, we never got caught.

Night Lights

Oak Ridge scientists were collecting fireflies. They were studying non-heat-producing light sources and they needed thousands of them. We called them "lightnin' bugs" and at the "first twinklin' o' the evenin'"we would grab our mason jars, grass in the bottom and air holes poked in the top, and set out to fill them up. Some children tried nets, but I preferred to catch them with my bare hand. Some folks put them in the freezer, but Cutch and I liked to keep ours on the screened-in porch. They were beautiful twinkling fairy lights. Then on Saturday mornings children would line up at the collection center to turn in our catch. We were paid a penny apiece if they were alive, and we were proud to be helping the scientists out at the Lab. We weren't told exactly what they were doing, but we understood; after all, we were used to secrets. Besides, a movie was only 25 cents so one jar could finance a whole lot of fun!

Croquet

Playing croquet at 108 Chatham was a challenge every summer. The "official" course consisted of little hills and valleys all up and down the giant steep hill that accompanied the 16 steps. You could hit the ball as hard as you could, but it would just roll back down. There were obstacles like a water drainage pipe, a sidewalk and a 4ft x 4ft cement slab located between our yard and the McKinstrys'. Its purpose was a mystery, but we were pretty sure it wasn't a grave marker. If an opponent "sent you away" with enough force, the ball could end up way down in the woods. There were no "out of bounds" markers, and no time limits, unless it got too dark to see the balls. Parents must have loved it, because it kept us occupied for hours.

Then Cutch and neighbor Doug began to figure things out. Their balls were finding little divots and staying put. It seems they were secretly digging out little ledges, enhancing nooks and crannies and practicing how to get those balls to stay on the hill. Then they began to challenge people to beat them at their own game. I don't think anyone ever did, and brother Cutch went on to become an excellent golfer, divots and all. And to think, he got his start on the hills of Chatham Lane! I'm sure he could have gone pro if he had chosen that path, but that's another story…

Sylvia

My mother did not like to iron. In the days before the words "permanent press" became a favorite part of her vocabulary, she hired Sylvia to do the job. Sylvia came once a week, on Tuesdays. On the nights before she came, Mother would dampen Dad's shirts for the week, along with a few other essential items and roll them up into balls. She took all the vegetables out of the drawers in the refrigerator and replaced them with these balls of cloth. The next morning she would set up the wooden ironing board in front of the TV in our small B-house living room, checking to make sure the fake vegetables were still damp. She refilled a special coke bottle with water and plugged in the iron. Sylvia arrived after lunch, just in time for the afternoon movie, which she watched while completing her task. The coke bottle served as a clothes sprinkler since steam irons were not yet on the market, at least not in Oak Ridge. Using an ice pick, Daddy had poked holes in the bottle top and clamped it back onto the water-filled coke bottle. Then Sylvia would shake it over the clothes and create steam as she ironed. Mother always made sure Sylvia had a real bottle of Coca-Cola on the side table in case she got thirsty. It always seemed to me that it would have been much easier for Mother to just iron the clothes herself, but that was not my call.

The Blue Room

Mr. and Mrs. Evans (Hal and Sue) lived next door to the McKinstrys, on the left-hand corner of Chatham Lane. They owned Ridge Beverage Sales on Warehouse Road. They were a well-loved and interesting couple. Sue was a sincere patriot. She admired and cared for her environment, her cats, and her fellow Americans. She generously shared her deepest thoughts and observations with those around her. The only problem was that in the passion of her elaborations she sometimes got her words

48

mixed up. Sue loved to stand out in her yard and philosophize with the neighbors. "Oak Ridge is so international," she would say, "It's just like Gatlinburg." She lamented about her dear cousin's daughter, who had to have an arboretum. Sue's cats were getting chubby. They needed more exorcism. And she didn't quite know what to think about Elvis Parsley. Hal, on the other hand, was more of a listener. Sometimes Mayor Mac and Doctor Moore would go down to Ridge Beverage for a beer after work. As the story goes, one time Dad came running out of the restroom shouting, "Hal, come quick! The toilet's turned blue!" Maybe he thought it was some sort of weird nuclear thing, affecting the water supply. "Oh that," replied Hal, in his calm sort of way, "Sue bought this new stuff called Ty-D-Bol. It cleans the commode and turns the water blue." From that day on, Ridge Beverage Sales became The Blue Room, where happy times meant more than just a bottle of beer.

Bootleggers

B houses were not very big, and cemesto walls were definitely not soundproof. So when the telephone on the kitchen wall rang in the middle of the night, it woke everybody up like an alarm clock. Anderson County was dry, which meant that you could not buy hard liquor of any kind within the city gates. There was a time when late at night, sometimes more than once, our phone would ring. Daddy would stumble to the kitchen, mumble, "wrong number," and shuffle back to bed. Phone would ring again. Same response. Then one night I heard him say, "Yes, a fifth of Jack Daniels and a Beefeater's Gin. Okay, got it." Then, next call, "Yep, they are on the way." This kept up for a few nights. Then he started adding things like,

49

"There's a two-for-one special on Old Grand-Dad." The next time it rang Mom was giggling and then I could hear them both snickering when he went back to bed. Turns out our phone number was one digit off from the local bootlegger's. Pretty soon our midnight caller got the message and nights were peaceful (boring!) again.

Rabbit Ears

Television was quite a novelty in the 1950's. Unlike today, the only channels we got at first were two networks, NBC and CBS. I loved to watch "Ramar of the Jungle", "Sea Hunt", and "Father Knows Best." Most of us girls had a huge crush on Tony Dow, so watching the classic "Leave It to Beaver" was absolutely mandatory. I don't remember much about American Bandstand and The Mickey Mouse Club and this puzzled me until later when Jane Ann reminded me that we didn't get their network, ABC, in the early years. Most likely the surrounding ridges were interfering with our rabbit ears. Even attaching strips of aluminum foil to the antennas didn't help. A definite deficit to my childhood days! Meanwhile, my dad would sometimes turn the channel to "Ole' Cas", who would open his show from Knoxville with ,"Hello neighbors, come on down and shop at the sign of the shears, and the name Cas Walker," or The Mulls Singing Convention ("This is the reverend, and Mrs. J. Bazzell Mull, (singing) Hello, everybody, How do you do...We've got entertainment, waiting for you..."), or Porter Waggoner and Dolly Parton. A voice from the kitchen would yell, "Dorie, turn that stuff off!" You see, my mother was more of a "Chattanooga Choo Choo", Glen Miller, "In the Mood", kind of girl.

Cas Walker later came on television and announced that fluoridated water was a Communist plot, hatched by "those people over in Oak Ridge." He wasn't very popular in the Secret City after that, but Dad always stayed partial to Dolly. Our neighbor Herb Ownby was her uncle and later when we girls worked a summer up in Gatlinburg, we rented rooms above Parton's Market. We were "Pearl's Girls", but that's another story...

Friday Night Football

Oak Ridge High School Wildcat Football was a Friday night tradition loved by all ages. My parents found a great way to watch the game, even when Cutch and I were way too young to sit still in the bleachers. Gorgas Lane, off of Georgia Avenue, ends on the hill up behind the visitors' bleachers on Blankenship Field. There were no tall trees back then to block the view. Our parents, along with Martha and Bill Wyatt (Bowden's brother) and other neighbors, would bring blankets and chairs down to the end of the Lane to watch the game while we children played behind them in the street. More Oak Ridge ingenuity! I learned to love the sounds of the fight song, "Roll, Wildcats, Roll!" at a very young age:

> Let's roll, Wildcats, roll!
> The fight is on, let's take it across the goal!
> Let's roll, Wildcats, roll!
> Your loyal sons are with you hundred fold!
> Rah! Rah! Rah!

Fight 'til the gun!
We'll cheer each play until the game is won!
Let's show 'em that we're tough!
Make 'em holler that's enough!
Yea, roll, Wildcats, roll!

Adlai vs. Ike

In the presidential election of 1956, my daddy was for
Adlai Stephenson and my mommy liked Ike. Every year
they cancelled each other's votes, yet still they voted. It
was both a duty and a privilege. You studied the facts, you
formed an opinion, and you voted. We were taught that it
was not respectful or polite to ask someone how they had
voted. Voting booths were secret for a very good reason.
If they wanted you to know, they would tell you. It made
sense because here in the Secret City, we were used to not
asking.   What a difference from the exit polls of today! I
remember going to Glenwood School wearing two big
campaign buttons, one supporting Stephenson, and one
supporting Eisenhower. The kids said I couldn't do that, I
had to make a choice. Didn't have to. I liked being fair,
and I wasn't old enough to vote.

Downtown

Here in Oak Ridge, we ARE a town, but we don't really
HAVE a town. There is no center city, with blocks lined
off for stores and such, like in other small towns such as
Cleveland, Tennessee, where I was born. I have to admit
that I did miss that atmosphere at times, but just like in so
many other areas, The Secret City is unique, and all things

52

considered, I wouldn't change our proud heritage one little bit.

In 1955, the Downtown Shopping Center opened and it did become the center of our city. It was huge, what today we would call a strip mall. Horseshoe-shaped with a giant parking lot in its center, it was our "down town." We shopped, ate at the cafeteria, held charity bake sales, sold Girl Scout cookies, and socialized. We learned to ride bicycles, drive cars, and parallel-park on the huge expanse of asphalt. Later, carnivals and circuses would set up on the parking lot and a row of in-ground trampolines bordered it on the Turnpike side.

Jonquils

Every spring, for as long as I can remember, The Daffodil Man came to town. Usually in early March, the Gilliams from Monteagle would bring in truckloads of beautiful yellow daffodils. Mr. Gilliam would set up shop in the parking lot and sell bunches of the sunny yellow trumpet-shaped flowers, also called jonquils, from the back of his pick-up truck. It was our harbinger of spring and we couldn't wait to take home that first bouquet. They also sold bags of bulbs to be planted, and most likely the jonquils we see growing around town in the spring had their beginnings in the back of Mr. Gilliam's truck. Almost anyone from Oak Ridge who has a birthday, anniversary, or any other special occasion in the early spring, will remember being honored with a bouquet of these beautiful blossoms. Today, as we drive out Pellisippi Parkway towards Knoxville or the airport, we are greeted each spring with (to quote the poet Wordsworth) "A Host of Golden Daffodils". Decorating each side of the highway, most likely at least some of these beauties are descendants of those who first arrived in the area on a truck with The Daffodil Man.

It may not have been a typical town, but Oak Ridge was OUR town. Today we are looking at a possible re-vitalization of our city center. Hopefully we, the second generation, can help to carry on the hopes and dreams and also the good times we shared with the first generation in this special place.

Santa and Spaghetti

Downtown Hardware anchored the lower east side of the Downtown Shopping Center. Owned and operated by the Clary family, it was the place to shop for tools and toys. There were no antiques and dusty aging do-dads as found in other small town hardware/general stores. Instead, there were aisles and aisles of tools, toys, gadgets, and gizmos. The clever engineers and creative scientists who had decided to stay on and fix up their cemestos needed all the latest products, and Tom Clary knew just how to accommodate them. Oak Ridgers were used to pitching in and working together, so on any given Saturday, you would see "the dads" gathering there, sharing ideas and giving advice. It was kind of our version of "gathering downtown on the courthouse steps." Only we also had Mrs. Wayman, in her bright red lipstick, greeting everyone with her signature, "Hello, Darlin'". Without family close by, for the holidays most Oak Ridgers either travelled or gathered with friends. I remember many Christmas Eves when Tom and Sadie Clary and the kids would come to our house for dinner. My mom's spaghetti was a tradition. It was delicious, plentiful, and would wait on anyone who suddenly had an unexpected "errand". Sometimes the phone would ring (remember, there were no cell phones) and it would be a frantic parent, looking for Tom Clary. It seems a child had added something important to the wish list, and did Tom perhaps have one in stock. No matter how late it was, Tom would jump in the car, open up the store, and find the item. Tom would tell them, "No need to pay, we'll just settle up later." And I'm sure they did. Meanwhile, it was Christmas Eve, and Tot's spaghetti was waiting on the stove.

Queen of the Night

Every year in late summer when the Night-blooming Cereus began to show signs of budding, party plans began. These spectacular plants, also called "Queen of the Night", bloom only once a year. The huge tropical blossoms begin to open around nine o'clock, slowly unfolding until they reach their saucer-size beauty around midnight. Daddy would prepare the backyard spotlight to shine just so, and mother would make the hors d'oeuvres. Hoping for weekend activity, friends and neighbors checked in often to track the status. When the buds began to show a soft pink, word would go out. Everyone came in their pajamas; a tradition in case it was a work night, and Mother Nature took our breath away. In bad weather the plants were brought up on the porch, and the show went on, rain or (moon)shine. The dirt floor "basement" under the house provided winter rest until they were returned to the edge of the woods the following spring.

Bookmobile

Once a week in the summer, the Bookmobile came to our neighborhood. Part of the Oak Ridge Public Library System, it was like a giant cave on wheels; wall to wall books, floor to ceiling. There was a full set of Laura Ingalls Wilder's Little House on the Prairie series, all the Nancy Drew Mysteries, the Oz books by L. Frank Baum, and Agatha Christies, for Mom. I loved it! The driver would even take requests, and try to have a special book on board to be checked out the following week. Applying for and obtaining our own personal library cards as children helped instill pride and a sense of responsibility, as well as a love of reading. If the books were not cared for, the cards were revoked. No second chances!

Most sunny afternoons brought us the musical ice cream truck down to the bottom of Chatham Lane. We could buy brown cows and creamsicles for five cents and popsicles in every flavor, even coconut. We sat on the concrete steps, enjoying our drippy treats, and then the sprinklers were turned on, and we ran through the water to rinse it all off. Those were the days!

Cool Clear Water

The Oak Ridge swimming pool is a giant cement pond, built by the U.S. Army Corps of Engineers in 1944. Covering 1.5 surface acres and holding 2.1 million gallons of water, it is among the biggest in the world. Completely spring-fed with crystal clear water, it is always very, very cold. I think it opened in the spring on Memorial Day weekend and remained open until September, when the young lifeguards had to return to college for classes in the fall.

Our parents could drop us off, confident in our safety. There were shower facilities, a snack bar, and a Red Cross first aid station. Supervision was provided by a dedicated city staff, along with ten or more lifeguards, mostly college students, stationed in their guard chairs along the perimeter of the pool and out on the raft in the center. We were not supposed to speak to them while on duty and the occasional megaphone warnings of "No running" and "Please stay off the ropes" were promptly obeyed or there would be time-out minutes in the grass.

"Inner tubes" of various sizes could be checked out like library books. No charge, just turn them in when finished. The giant ones could hold five or six kids and what fun we had trying to stand up, hold hands, and balance on the ring. The Red Cross provided free swimming lessons on Saturday mornings. Learning to swim out to the raft (water over our heads) was a monumental task, and a proud accomplishment. Many of my friends went on to competitive swimming with the Atomic City Aquatic Club (ACAC) but I was happy just to cheer them on.

Radioactive Dimes

A visit to the Atomic Energy Museum was always a must whenever company came to town. It opened in 1949 on the exact same day that the armed guard stations surrounding the city came down, and has continually evolved and grown along with our ever-expanding scientific community. I remember playing with radioactive dimes. You dropped your dime into a large isotope cabinet in the lobby of the

57

museum. The machine would process the dime and return it, full of radioactivity, yet safely enclosed in a special souvenir coin holder. My guess is that they really weren't all that safe, because that exhibit can no longer be found at the Museum, and the dimes are difficult to find, even in yard sales.

The most impressive exhibit I remember is still popular today. The Van DeGraff generator resembles a large silver ball, balanced on top of a pedestal. You place your hand on the ball, and no matter how long your hair is, it stands straight up on top of your head. As the scientific theory was explained, we were told it was a force that could kill us, but fortunately it never did! Today, our newly-named American Museum of Science and Energy (AMSE) is a great place to take grandchildren and is still a must-see for anyone who visits the Secret City.

Whippoorwill

Big Ridge State Park is part of the Great Smokey Mountains National Forest. Located about 40 miles from Oak Ridge, it was our favorite recreation spot for many years. Ranger Robb was in charge of the park for most of those years and we kids got to know him very well. Maybe too well, on certain occasions! He took his job seriously, and his rules were meant to be followed, even if we didn't always completely agree with them. The heavily wooded forest was an ideal setting for Girl Scout Camp Whippoorwill.

Big Ridge is a small quiet lake, nestled along the top of a small dam in TVA's Norris Lake system. If you paddle a canoe to the rim, the only thing preventing toppling on over is a (we thought very flimsy) metal screen. The view was, and still is, amazing.

Camp Whippoorwill was my first overnight out of town venture away from the family. We stayed for a whole week, in small cabins of four bunks each. We had to use flashlights at night to get to the common latrine down the hill. The "buddy system" was in full effect, so if the facilities were needed, a bunkmate had to wake up and go along. Thoughts of snakes, bears, and hoot-owls provided a great incentive to wait until first light in the morning. Meals were served in the main dining hall, but an occasional hot dog was grilled "out in the wild" over an open campfire, which we Scouts learned how to accomplish "the old-fashioned way" (no matches).

We lashed logs to build stair steps for erosion control, dug latrines, and learned to safeguard our snack bags from bears by hanging them from tree branches. We studied and conserved nature. Ranger Robb was very proud. We also identified poison ivy (leaves of three, let it be) and learned to apply calamine lotion liberally as needed. We did not like bugs. Evenings around the campfire were filled with songs, skits and stories of all sorts. Scary, silly, heartwarming and educational, we loved them all. The song "Kumbaya" was a current hit on the radio, and we also loved "Found a Peanut", "Cannibal King", "Davey Crockett", "On Top of Old Smokey", and "Que Sera, Sera", just to name a few. We were enthralled with stories of the Cherokee Indians, trying to imagine what it was really like for a young Indian squaw and her papoose, in these same woods so long ago. There were crafts, games, and sports of all kinds. I loved archery and canoe lessons and anything to do with the water.

One Thursday afternoon, having just mastered the art of a high arched-back dive, I misjudged the distance along the pier and dove head-first into four feet of water. Lifeguards thought my neck was broken. An ambulance quickly arrived and rushed me to the Oak Ridge Hospital Emergency Room. By the time my frantic family arrived, I was laughing with the nurse and begging to return to camp. Dr. Preston had heard of my accident and rushed from his rounds to come and check on me. Mother was reluctant to let me go back, but dear Dr. Preston, with a wink and a hug, convinced her otherwise.

I was welcomed back by a large crowd of my fellow Girl Scouts. Knowing I had to be carefully watched, they proclaimed me "Princess Taliaferro" and constructed an elaborate "throne" out at the end of the pier, so I could look out over my subjects as they frolicked in the lake. I loved the honor and attention, but I would much rather have been swimming.

I will always remember last night at Camp Whippoorwill. We gathered at dusk along the dock for our farewell ceremony and to sing our camp song one more time:

> Gone to bed is the setting sun.
> Night is coming and day is done.
> Whippoorwill, Whippoorwill,
> Has just begun.

As our young voices echoed out across the silent lake in front of us, darkness was creeping in. Flickering torches began to appear along the far shore. Canoes were rippling through the water towards us. As the torch-lit canoes came closer, the skies grew darker, and soon we could make out their images in the firelight. The canoes were filled with Indians, emerging before us in full Cherokee dress, face paint, feathers and spears. The Chief was standing majestically at the bow, flaming torch in hand, his feather headdress seemingly in flames around him. Braves paddled canoes behind him. The sounds of beating drums and rhythmic chanting grew louder, the closer they came. We were mesmerized and this beautiful authentic pageant instilled in our young minds a truly enduring appreciation of the Cherokee Nation. Through the coming years I spent a lot of time at Big Ridge, but none can compare with this week at Camp Whippoorwill. Thank you, Ranger Robb.

Fake Surfing

Big Ridge wasn't the only lake we had close by. Norris Lake was much larger. We often took Jackie Seagull's speed boat out to Andersonville Boat Dock where we perfected our water-skiing skills. We learned to slalom and take off from the dock. Even though I never considered myself an athlete, I was a pretty good water skier. Some of the boys learned to ski barefoot, but that was way too much for me.

Lots of Oak Ridge families owned cabins out on Watts Bar Lake. Since it was only about 30 minutes away, we spent many summer hours there. We loved playing volleyball, boating, swimming, water-skiing, partying and "homemade surfing" over the wake with friends such as David Culver, Arthur Snell, Diehl Unger, Dale Blanco and lots of others. Thanks to all the families for providing both food for us and fuel for the boats!

One weekend Arthur Snell invited us out to a big house party at his family's cabin on Watts Bar. There were 30 or more of us teenagers hanging out all weekend and staying up all night. Dicky Ramsey gave us a huge scare. We were sitting in a speed boat and Dicky was in the water back by the motor. Suddenly the engine started up. We couldn't see Dicky and were sure his legs had gotten caught in the blades. Actually, he had been smart enough to dive deep under the water. When he finally surfaced, he was okay and we continued our awesome house party until late Sunday afternoon. Hopefully we helped the Snells with clean-up afterward, but I kind of doubt that we did. We were invited back again, so apparently all was well.

Dancin' Fools

Dancing played a big part in the Oak Ridge social scene in the fifties and sixties. There were tea dances, patio parties, and formals at the Oak Ridge Country Club, as well as dinner dances, sock hops, sweet sixteen parties (Madelyn Lundin's dance at the Holiday Inn and Carolyn Hensley's at the Starlight Room), home parties, like Judy Lane's dance on her backyard tennis court, and Tappie Corbin's party when sister Pattie and I spied on them "sleepwalking"on the patio. We danced at Donnie Baby's, the Peppermint Lounge, the Wildcat Den and the Armory. There were Country Club Dances, Civic Club Dances, Teen Board Dances, Hullabaloos, Winter Formals, TWIRP dances, Sadie Hawkins Day dances, Christmas dances, Proms, Dogwood Balls, Social Club Formals, Cotillion Presentations, and the Cotton Ball, just to name a few. We danced to live bands like The Clef Dwellers from the high school, The Embers. Rex and the Galaxies, The Satellites, The Twilighters, The Sierras, The True-Tones, Herbie Osborne's Combo, The Esquires, The Clansmen, Dog Man Dan Morgan and Co., The Blenders, The Deltas, The Apollos, The Jades, Dale and the Del-Hearts, The Martells, and The Earls, featuring Gordon Rhea on the drums. I probably left some out, but definitely not on purpose. Jim Clark was our DJ from WATO and whenever he played for any occasion, he knew just what records to spin.

We danced "The Jerk", "The Pony", "The Stroll", "Doin' the Dog", and the "Mashed Potatoes." We slow-danced to "Wonderland by Night" and anything Johnny Mathis. Even gym class required square dancing, combining boys and girls classes to learn steps that would " really come in handy" like the Virginia Reel, Pickin' up Paw- paws, Do-si-do, The Grand March, and the Hokey Pokey (What if that really is what it's all about?)

Ethel Howell Dance Lessons

My parents wanted me to learn the social graces, so I, along with many other second generation children, began ballroom dance classes in the fifth grade. Miss Margaret Marrs, one of the original Oak Ridge High School teachers, started a dance class in the 1940's as a Student Council after-school activity. It became so popular that Mrs. Ethel Howell gradually took it over and formed the Ethel Howell Dance Studio. She taught us to waltz, beginning with the box step (step, side, together), fox trot (slow, slow, side together, slow), jitterbug (1-2-3, 1-2-3, rock back) and cha-cha (I don't remember the exact sequence, but it was sort of a "create it as you go and hope Mrs. Howell approves" kind of dance).

She held formal dinner dances at the Oak Terrace Ballroom, next to the bowling alley in Grove Center, so that we could put our skills to the test. All students could attend, "stag or drag", but couples were encouraged. At this young age, partners were called "escorts", not "dates". The boys were taught the proper way to ask for a date and to ask for a dance, and the girls were taught how to accept. Declining was discouraged. However, if we did decline one invitation, we were not allowed to accept another. There were corsages, boutonnieres, dinner jackets, and white gloves. For many of us girls it was the first pair of (not really so high) heels.

Mrs. Howell was very strict about manners and social protocol. The reasoning was that if ever invited to the White House for dinner, Oak Ridgers were expected to know how to behave. Finger tip bowls were not filled with lemonade. For those of you who, like myself, do not dine frequently at State Dinners in Washington, finger bowls are provided for each guest at a formal table. They are small shallow bowls filled with lemon water for gently dipping finger tips, in case one encounters a bit of sauce before using the cloth napkin. Traditionally a thin slice of lemon is floated on top so that it is not embarrassingly mistaken for a bowl of clear soup.

Once when I was little, we went on vacation to Florida. We stopped for dinner along the way, and didn't realize it was such an upscale fancy restaurant until we were already seated. So three-year-old Cutch and I had not had any warnings about manners and my parents were a little nervous. We were all too hungry to drive any further to find a more family-friendly restaurant, and since fast-food establishments like McDonald's had not yet appeared on the scene, formality seemed our best option. The first thing I did was ask the tuxedo-clad waiter why they served their lemonade in bowls instead of glasses and could I please have a straw. There was an awkward silence for a few seconds, then soft laughter, and, crisis averted, a good time was had by all. The waiter brought my fried shrimp, along

with homemade lemonade for everyone, "on the house."
An appreciation of gracious living, and its accompanying
good manners, remained important to the Secret City's first
generation, and Mrs. Howell taught their children well.

Chicken fingers

Fried chicken was eaten with knife and fork, according to
Mrs. Howell, and never with the fingers. Maybe she
wanted us to acquire that particular dining skill, so fried
chicken appeared on the menu for the formal Christmas
Dance. That's when the Great Chicken Controversy began.
An advice column titled "Dear Abby" appeared in the Oak
Ridger. Abby (Abigail Van Buren) declared it perfectly
acceptable to eat fried chicken with the fingers, as long as
the bones were placed properly, to the upper left side of the
plate. Sacrilege! Parents and children took sides.
Whatever shall we do? Ethel Howell would have none of
that nonsense, so she immediately changed the menu.
Problem solved! Clearly, the term "chicken fingers" had an
entirely different meaning in those days.

Bo

One of my sixth grade escorts was good friend Bo Spitzer.
His parents, Ed and Peggy, owned the very first Oak Ridge
Dairy Queen, located on the corner of California Avenue
and the Oak Ridge Turnpike. Oak Ridgers loved the cones
of soft-swirled vanilla ice cream, especially when hand-
dipped in chocolate or butterscotch, and there were often
long lines of customers, waiting patiently to place their
orders at the outside window.

On the night of our dance, Bo arrived at the door, all dressed up in a white dinner jacket, with a pretty white cardboard box in his hand. It was my first corsage, pink carnations! Feeling like almost teenagers (we were eleven), we climbed the sixteen steps up to the street where Bo's dad was waiting to drive us to the Oak Terrace. Standing at the top of the hill, we looked all around the lane, but the car was nowhere to be seen. Apparently, Peggy had told Ed to take Bo to Tollie's house. She forgot to tell him to wait and take us to the dance! But all was well. Daddy put Bo at ease, happily drove us to the dance, and we had a wonderful time.

On to Donnie Baby's

Live bands played at most of these occasions, and Mrs. Howell was always in charge of the playlist. The girls were given dance cards, little decorated paper booklets with small pencils attached with matching chorded ribbons. The inside pages were printed with numbers and spaces for each official dance. Boys asked for dances and signed the card, but the first and last dances were traditionally reserved for the escort. My mother saved my cards, and names like Richard Greer, John Tighe, Charles Niemeier, Jeff Smiley, Tommy Spray, Parker Stanley, Lee Ruch, Boyd Davis, K.C. Jones, Tatum Fowler, Dwight Foster, Kurt Strasser, and Steve Kwasnoski really do bring back the memories!

One Year Mrs. Howell took a high school competition dance formation team to New York City. They appeared one morning on the Today show and they danced at the World's Fair. They were exceptionally talented and skillful and these second generation dancers made their Secret City proud!

In 1962 when Donnie Baby's Teenage Nightclub came to town, it was bye-bye jitterbug and hello, rock and roll! Cha-lypso and the Pelvis Knock were the new dance sensations. The club was located near Jackson Square. After much discussion, I was allowed to go, but it always seemed there were more parents standing along the walls than there were kids dancing, and it didn't last very long.

Nucular Physicist

Adults did a lot of dancing back then as well. Weekends were always busy at the Country Club, and various divisions at Union Carbide and AEC had dance parties, formals, and holiday festivities throughout the year. One year a couple from Cleveland came up to attend the ORNL (Oak Ridge National Laboratory) Nuclear Division Gala with Mom and Dad. Apparently the husband was a big talker and liked to "enhance" the facts from time to time. Determined to fit in with the Oak Ridge crowd, he proudly announced that he, too, was a nucular physicist. Not NUCLEAR, but NUCULAR. His pronunciation was a dead give-away to everyone. He was clearly "not from 'round here". Without missing a beat, the crowd kept up the charade all night, using all kinds of made-up scientific terms and supposedly even confiding atomic "secrets" as the night went on. As the story goes, it was the best dance ever, especially for the Cleveland guests.

I often wonder, considering all this dancing experience we have, why no one from The Secret City has yet appeared on "Dancing with the Stars"!

Bleeding Madras

Living close to Knoxville, our family always loved
Tennessee Volunteer Football. Daddy once said that on
Saturdays in the fall, even his blood turned orange. Mother
arranged fall flowers and orange candles on the mantle,
interspersed with various Vol paraphernalia, and Orange
Blossoms were her "cocktail du jour."

Every third Saturday in October UT plays Alabama. One
year, Mom and Dad's good friends from Cleveland, Bird
and Preacher Sloan, frequent visitors to Oak Ridge and
huge fans of the Crimson Tide, came up for the big game.
The four of them had grown up together and Dad was their
son Steve's godfather. Everyone dressed up for games
back then, so the ladies were in dresses and heels. Daddy
put on his best white shirt and brand new Madras sports
coat. Madras fabric was high style back then. The tag
(which he probably didn't read) explained that "These
native dyes are used in excess. With each washing, the
dyes run somewhat into the water…this 'bleeeding' gives
your garment its distinctively muted and subdued colorings,
characteristic of authentic India madras." Midway through
the football game, it started to rain. Umbrellas are not
allowed at Neyland Stadium, and by the time they got
home, they were drenched. Daddy's khaki pants looked as
if they were tye-died, and his white shirt was dripping
stripes of purple, magenta, red, yellow, turquoise and
chartreuse. I have no idea who won the game. I was afraid
to ask, but the sports coat was looking very authentic.

Steve Sloan played football at the University of Alabama
and after rooming with Joe Namath, went on to quarterback
the Crimson Tide to the 1964 Orange Bowl Championship.
I am guessing that Daddy's blood was a lot more red than

orange on that game day. Later when Cutch quarterbacked the Oak Ridge Wildcats, Daddy's red blood was half gray, and then the University of Kentucky turned it to a bright shade of blue, but that's another story...

Jefferson Junior High

By the time I went to junior high school (1959), Jefferson was located in the original Oak Ridge High School building, facing Kentucky Avenue above Blankenship Field. The new high school at its current location on Providence road was built by the Atomic Energy Commission in 1951. The term "middle school" was not yet being used. There were two junior high schools, grades seven through nine, in the Secret City. Competition was very strong! Robertsville, the red and white Rams, served the western part of the city, and Jefferson served the East. According to the JJHS handbook of 1960, the school colors are blue and gold and the official emblem is an eagle, clutching an atomic bomb in its claws. The booklet also included a civil defense plan, to be implemented as a result of enemy action.

The government still played a large part in funding our schools and they were excellent. Teachers and staff went through a tough screening process and I really believe we had the cream of the crop. Learning was fun, sports were prolific, and social life was fabulous.

Snewpys

Our newspaper, The Jefferson Eagle, was printed on ditto paper in purple ink. We knew the paper was being printed when the distinctive smell of the ink came drifting down the halls. The cost was three cents per copy. We were early entrepreneurs, and in eighth grade, we raised the cost to four cents. Along with the help of our editor, Barbara Spangler, we expressed opinions, gossiped, made jokes, reported on club activities and athletics, and occasionally commented on non-school news. "Snewpys," the gossip column, (author undisclosed), was full of initials, abbreviations and code words. To the students it was like reading our own version of shorthand. We knew exactly what it all meant, and we hoped the adults would not bother to try and de-code it. Anyway, by the time it was deciphered, "whoever" would have a new boyfriend or girlfriend anyway.

There were contests, riddles, class news, PTA reports, and jokes. One example of junior high school humor back in the day referred to the girl who bought a book entitled, How to Hug, and discovered she had purchased Vol. 9 of the encyclopedia! Jennifer Frame wrote an article urging more responsible use of the school suggestion box. Requests such as "Get rid of Mrs. So and So", "Down with Tests" and complaining about the cafeteria food won't help anyone, she said;we need to be more grown up. Sandy Shapiro complained about behavior in the cafeteria and suggested holding an assembly to address this problem. Putting hands in other people's food and yelling across the table were bad ideas, she reported.

School Songs

Our Alma Mater, written by instrumental music teacher, Miss Alice Lyman, was always sung in assemblies and at ballgames. An article in the Eagle urged more participation, and even questioned the patriotism of the student body because not everyone knew the words. Anyone who was around the school during this time will probably at least be familiar with our Alma Mater:

> Here's to you our Alma Mater, Jefferson, Jefferson
> Guide us in our loyalty to all we hold most dear.
> We who through your portals enter,
> Jefferson, Jefferson
> Know that fortune smiles upon us here.
> Teach us to be wise and strong
> Help us know the right from wrong.
> While we weave into a song
> Words of praise for you…Oh,
> Here's to you our Alma Mater, Jefferson, Jefferson
> Proudly we your gold and blue now bear.

And I bet you are even more familiar with the Pep Song:

> Jefferson Junior High's the school we cheer for,
> Jefferson Junior High, we sing to you
> Jefferson is just the place to be
> For sportsmanship and loyalty,
> Jefferson we will see you through, Rah! Rah! Rah!
> Look at that keen ball team how they are fighting.
> Hear how the band can play a peppy tune.
> We'll all pull together, no matter what the weather
> From September until June.

Hissy Fits

Mrs. Clara Walsh was a very memorable seventh grade teacher. She taught penmanship as if it were calculus. "Your signature represents who you are," she would say;

71

"Be proud of it." We were graded on our oval wheels and speed writing. Sometimes she would get exasperated over something (passing notes, giggling, hiding comic books inside our textbooks, and other seventh grade stuff) and would announce to the class, "Ooooh, I'm going to have a hissy fit!" and then she would. Have a hissy fit, that is. After a few moments of shaking both hands simultaneously in front of her shoulders as fast as she could, things would suddenly become calm again. I always wondered how she kept the fingers on one hand from smacking into those on the other hand. It was an art, and she perfected it. The Art of the Hissy Fit.

Mrs. Walsh loved wild flowers and was a true expert on most anything growing naturally in our area. In the spring of 1960 she took us on a field trip to the woods up on the hills behind the Garden Apartments (now Rolling Hills Apartments, across the Turnpike from the Armory). We had to climb through a barbed wire fence along the ridge, like secret agents on a clandestine mission. As Oak Ridgers, we of course loved anything "secret". If we were not supposed to be there, she didn't say so, and we knew not to ask.

Could this be where the probably non-existent, mutated, two-headed monsters lived? Mrs. Walsh knew where to show us beautiful lady's slipper orchids, wild ginger pots, trillium, Japanese iris and May apples. It was nature's fairyland, invisible unless you knew where to find it. Years later, thinking back, I suspect she was also working for the government, observing flora and reporting any changes, monitoring effects the Manhattan Project could be having on our natural habitat. Now, back to the barbed wire. Remember, I am not the athletic one of the group. Climbing back through the fence, I scraped my leg on the rusty wire and made a four-inch gash on the back of my calf. It required a trip to the emergency room. As I was leaving, a classmate whispered, "Don't tell anyone where you have been…" I was more concerned with the giant needle destined to deliver my tetanus shot. No stitches required, but to this day I still have the jagged scar, proof of our secret adventure.

Tear Jerker

Since 1944 the Ridge Movie Theater was located next to Service Drug Store in Jackson Square. It was a popular place on weekends, especially for the junior high school crowd. On Fridays, a note might circulate through the classrooms and whisper through the halls, "Ridge Theater, 7:10." Even though we had no texting apparatus, the message flew, and we arrived on schedule, en masse.

One particular night, just as the movie was over, the pick-up parade inched closer. Family cars lined up all down Broadway, past The Music Box, through the Square, even past the library on the corner and winding down towards the Alexander Inn. As the exits opened, a river of children quickly flowed through the doors. As we emerged, suddenly brakes screeched, car doors flung open and as word spread, parents began running frantically towards us. We girls were sobbing hysterically and the boys were consoling us. Panic ensued. Everyone talked at once until finally the grown-ups realized we had just watched the movie, "Gone With The Wind". Bonnie Blue had died and Rhett left Scarlet standing at the door. Tears soon turned to laughter and, crisis averted, what fun we all had!

We learned a lesson that night on the effects of really good drama and we could not wait until Monday morning when our own version began. We re-enacted the movie, every chance we could, for days, maybe even weeks. Ralph Armstrong was most often Rhett Butler and David Johnson was Ashley Wilkes. We girls took turns being Scarlet O'Hara, Melanie, and other characters, working to get our exaggerated accents just right. Kinstry's near-perfect impression of Prissy's "Oh Miss Scah-lit, I don't know nothin' 'bout birthin' babies," was hysterical. It kept us laughing for months, and I am sure it still would, even today.

Speaking Up

Mrs. Erma Neff taught us drama and public speaking. We memorized and recited works by Robert Frost, James Whitcomb Riley, Emily Dickenson and Omar Khayyam, just to name a few. We competed in dramatic readings and we studied Shakespeare. There was a competition during assembly in which contestants presented a dramatic reading or monologue, either humorous or serious. The title of mine was "Lawdy, Miss Clottie", a funny spoof about a young clueless parlor maid who goes to see the serious Shakespeare play "Othello" and returns to tell her lady all about it. Her rendition of her misinterpretations was hilarious. Mrs. Neff helped us choose really good pieces and she spent time coaching us, even after school. The judges, professors from the University of Tennessee School of Dramatic Arts, met with us later in class to discuss the performances and give us helpful advice going forward. They said I would have won first place but I didn't pause long enough for the laughter to subside and some of my words were lost to the audience. Let the record show, I did not sing!

Mrs. Neff emphasized elocution and when she presented her rendition of Rudyard Kipling's long 1903 poem, "Boots", you could hear a pin drop:

Foot—foot—foot—foot—sloggin' over Africa–
Boots—boots—boots—boots—
Movin' up and down again–
There's no discharge in the war!

I don't think elocution is emphasized much anymore. She also taught us to debate. Ironically, my major debate topic was "Resolved: That the United States government should provide federal aid to education for all public schools." We drew straws, and I was on the negative team, which meant I had to do my best to tear down the concept. This was quite a challenge to us, members of the second generation, whose education had been almost entirely at the expense of the United States Government! Mrs. Neff was a strict teacher, but she was fair. One of her favorite quotations, from Shakespeare's "Hamlet", has remained mine as well:

"This above all, to thine own self be true...
Thou canst not then be false to any man."

High Voltage

The only time I ever got a C at Jefferson was one second quarter in Glendon Jackson's science class. It was well deserved, because at that time, giggling and not paying attention were more important to the class than studying. Mr. Jackson had his hands full. Handsome in his own way, he wore pastel button-down shirts, crisply ironed, and shiny black patent-leather loafers. He was always clean-shaven and his jet-black hair was perfectly slicked back with

Brylcreem. The class would get out of control at the least little thing, and when he stomped his foot, hands on hips, and repeated the famous, "Now, Class…", we pretty much ignored him. That went on until someone laid down the law, and grades improved dramatically after that.

The following story, written by Henry Feldman in the Jefferson Eagle, is a good example of some of our science escapades:

"As a nine-weeks project, one of Mr. Jackson's science students constructed an electrical circuit controlled by light…when the ambitious electrician passed his hand in front of the photocell, it would set off a phonograph record that contained nothing but uproarious, ear-splitting laughter. Just as our mad scientist triggered the gadget, the door opened and in walked (our principal) Mr. Wallace Spray and a dignified –looking visitor, who were immediately greeted by wild, hysterical laughter from the record player. Mr. Spray looked slightly embarrassed, the dignified guest was immeasurably rattled, and Mr. Jackson turned a beautiful shade of purple, while the entire class contributed to double the amount of laughter in the room."

Miss Lyman

I wasn't a music student, but I appreciated all our music programs, especially the Jefferson band and orchestra. We all owe a special tribute to the legendary Alice Lyman. Since my musical friends seemed in awe of her and slightly more than afraid of her, I guess I was too. Stories of flying erasers and loud stern admonishments resulted in pride and excellence. Miss Lyman demanded perfection and Oak Ridgers were proud to oblige. She was our music, and she wrote the words. Later when my family owned Tot and Tollie's Flower Shop, we heard Miss Lyman play the organ for many, many Oak Ridge weddings. She could often be seen, walking about town, humming, or whistling softly to herself. She was an Oak Ridge treasure.

Hail, Caesar!

Phase one of my Latin education began in ninth grade. It was a required subject if we were to be doctors, and lawyers, and such, and of course scientists. It has been greatly beneficial to me through the years, especially in answering questions on "Jeopardy!" Mr. James Q. Webber, Chairman of the Tennessee Junior Classical League, and affectionately known as "Jimmy Q", was our Latin teacher and Latin Club sponsor. Latin was a tough subject, and Mr. Webber did his best to make it interesting.

In December of ninth grade, we had a party in the gym. Dressed in our togas, sandals, and appropriate Roman attire, we held a slave auction as the main event. The auctioneer, Malcolm Richardson, stirred up so much enthusiasm that some slaves went for as much as $6.00, and we made $34.90 for our upcoming Roman banquet in the spring. The year before we only produced a total of $7.50.

For entertainment, some of the boys volunteered for gladiator fights. While Steve Stelzman announced them, the audience signified "thumbs up" or "thumbs down." The gladiators were John Lyell, Jeff Smiley, Steve Elbert, and Jerry Hunt. The epic film, "Spartacus" came out in 1960. It starred Kirk Douglas as a rebellious Roman slave, and we Latin students loved it. Every so often, one of our "slaves" would jump to his feet, shouting, "I am

Spartacus!" Another would follow him shouting, "No, I am Spartacus!" Then everyone would shout together in unison, "We are Spartaci!" This spontaneous outbreak could happen at any time, no matter when or where we were. We had to make Latin interesting, somehow!

We elected our Latin Club officers: consuls, censors, tribunes, quaesters, aediles Eurulis, and aediles Plebeii; then we spent the rest of the evening on important things, like talking (in English), and twisting, continentaling, doing the "limbo", and practicing the popular dance "Madison Time."

The spring banquet was an authentic Roman feast, complete with a huge pig, roasted on a spit, and presented to Caesar by slaves, carrying it to him in a large procession. We spent weeks getting our costumes, decorations, and the menu just right. School officials and dignitaries, including Mayor Bissell, were our guests of honor.

In April Mr. Webber took us to the State Latin Convention. We spent the weekend at the Drake Hotel in Nashville. The Convention was held at Vanderbilt University, where we enacted Roman Forums, and participated in various Roman activities. Sessions started with everyone saying the Pledge of Allegiance in Latin. We also pledged to "Hand on the torch of classical civilization in the modern world." We visited the Parthenon, and roamed around the campus in our sandals and togas. Veni, vidi, vici: we came, we saw, we conquered!

Lavadava

We JJHS students not only studied Latin, but we also spoke
a special language of our own. Far better than even Pig
Latin, it was Lavadava Talk. We carried on conversations
that to others were pure gibberish, but we girls understood
every word. Now, 53 years later, the secret is finally being
told. You take the first consonant of every syllable, add av
to it, then pronounce the rest of the syllable. If the syllable
begins with a vowel, av precedes it. My name was
Tavollavie Mavoore. I lived in AvOak Ravidge
Tavennavesavee. Avit wavas favun. It drove our parents
crazy and when others began to catch on, we switched to
Suppenduppie. Same idea, but new sound. Today my
eight year-old grandson Joshua is fluent in Lavadava, and
he enjoys carrying on the tradition of driving his mother
"the nuts"!

Four no-trump, doubled and re-doubled

Playing bridge was one of our passions in junior high. We
girls played whenever and wherever we could. My mother
was a Life Master and she and the other moms helped out
and played with us whenever they could. Sandy, Gage,
Krattler, Anne, Kinstry, Ellen and I were the usual group,
along with anyone else we could get to join us. Eating and
talking were just as important as the actual card games. We
had homemade chocolate chip cookies (Selma would let us
eat the raw cookie dough), potato chips with homemade
onion dip (Lipton's dry onion soup mix and sour cream),
smoked oysters and sometimes shrimp with cocktail sauce,
and Mrs. Frye's famous fudge pie. There was always a
case of Cokes in the Ergen basement and Marie Gardiner's

kitchen produced all kinds of wonderful treats. The rest of us contributed assorted goodies whenever we could.

There were a lot of traditions and superstitions associated with our bridge games, but we got really serious once the bidding began. Dummy had to check on refreshments and could not even glance into anyone's hand of cards. Peeking over shoulders was strictly forbidden. It was good luck to sit parallel to the bath tub. We always tried to get Anne talking so she would be distracted, but she had this uncanny ability to talk a mile a minute and still keep track of every card in everybody's hands. I think it runs in the family, but that's another story...

Kingston Trio records often played in the background and when we wanted a break, Krattler would bring out her bass ukulele and we would sing along to songs like" Bondua", "Stewball", " 26 Miles (Santa Catalina)" and" The Seine". We played duets of "Heart and Soul" on the piano and we "Shuffled off to Buffalo."

Startime

One summer night we changed Kinstry's back yard into "Startime", a talent extravaganza, hosted by our favorite master of ceremonies, classmate John Lyell. It was a packed house, with standing room only, and even our concrete steps were full of fans. The first act was Judy "All Go Crazy" Lane, singing her version of "Everglades". The tin cup attached to her ukulele was to catch pennies as they were thrown her way. Others following her were Linda "The Voice" McKinstry, singing "Blue Moon", the "Miscellaneous Beauties", featuring, among others, Anne Dickey Browning, Linda Miller, Mary DePersio and Judy

Lane, singing "Does Your Chewing Gum Lose its Flavor on the Bedpost Overnight", "The Sisters Four", comprised of Thurmon Whitson, John Lyell, and Glen Beckham, singing "Blood and Whiskey", and "The Three of Us", Judy Lane and Linda McKinstry, performing their world-famous rendition of "Dream Baby". "The Rickets", Glen Beckham and Kinstry danced a soft-shoe routine while crooning "Give My Regards to Broadway." The Grand Finale was an all-sing, "500 Miles". The audience was enthralled with the great variety of voices and faces appearing in the show. Actually, I think my parents and Linda's, peeking out from behind curtains at the windows, had the best seats in the house!

NMCTASIH

We had opinions about most everything, and Gage's favorite expression was, "Heavens to Murgatroid." It was a great comment, heard often, but I always wondered, what or who the heck was Murgatroid? Finding out had NMCTASIH, a favorite saying to write on our spiral notebooks, and I still don't know. Gary Patterson amazed us with his piano playing and we had Hootenannys out by the lake. I wonder what it would have been like if we had had karaoke back then!

We wrote comments in spiral-bound stenographer's notebooks and passed them around the halls and classrooms at Jefferson. Numbers were assigned to those writing comments and to those who were being commented upon. It was similar to what you might write in a yearbook, only brief. Phrases like "cute", "funny", "love her", and so forth quickly filled the pages, which everyone could see. Keeping them away from the eyes and hands of teachers was not easy, but I managed to hold on to one, which I still have today!

Looking back, it seems that a disproportionate amount of our social times revolved around food. Progressive dinners made us feel very "avant-garde". It was "soup to nuts" and required at least five people. We would go house to house, with a different course at each one. Parents would drop us off at the appetizer house, then appetizer mom or dad would drive us to the salad house, salad house would take us to the soup house, and so on. If more people wanted to join in, we just added more courses!

Fads

Something about living here in the South kept us from being first in fashion, music, fads, trends, and all things New York or California. We were not hillbillies; we didn't even know what that meant. It wasn't because of secrets or gates. We had our Villagers, Wejuns, and Capezios; it's just that trendy things never seemed to get to us first. However, one fad finally did reach us in 1965. Annie Swope got her ears pierced!

Loveman's Department Store, Samuels, and Nettie Lee had nice dresses and such. But the highest fashions were in those fancy dress boxes that Selma ordered from Bonwit Teller in Boston and hid under Sandy's bed so Ted wouldn't know how much she had bought. Gage's dad travelled to Texas and bought her a scarab bracelet from Neiman-Marcus Department Store in Dallas. We were so impressed! Scarab jewelry was high-style, and the exotic stones were designed from fossilized Egyptian beetles, which does sound a little odd, but they are beautiful. We loved collecting charms for our sterling silver charm bracelets and gave them to each other to commemorate all sorts of special occasions and events. Along with those of my mother's, from her younger days, my charms now fill four bracelets and I love sharing stories of each one with friends and grandchildren. Wonderful memories!

The Music Box in Jackson Square had little private booths with ear phones so we could listen to a record before we bought it. But still, we needed to know what kids in other parts of the country were listening to. Sometimes very late on a clear night we could tune in DJ Dick Biondi (WLS Chicago) on the radio, or even WBZ Boston, after Knoxville's WNOX signed off earlier in the evening. Reception was staticky on our little transistor radios, but well worth it, in our teenage world.

Athleticism

I loved going to all the ballgames, but gym class was not my thing. You see, Cutch got all the tall, athletic genes, and I got the short asthmatic ones. 72 steep steps separated the Jefferson gym from Blankenship Field below. In seventh grade gym class, I passed out, halfway around the cinder track, trying to run the 440. Then I had to face those monstrous steps to get back up to school. Coach Bobbie Smith got me through it, and helped me understand that not everyone was an athlete, but at least I should try. I was still worried about my gym grade.

President Kennedy's Fitness Program didn't help much either. We stood behind a line and threw a softball. Mine went maybe a few feet, but teaching me to throw seemed to have little importance. Someone just measured the distance and recorded the numbers. Must have been a girl thing, back then.

Shadda-lump-dump

We girls tried to play tennis. We did not like playing in the hot sun, and our outfits were probably more important than our skills. After sun down we liked to go to the tennis courts in Jackson Square. We bounced our balls against the wooden back stop which is still there today, and called it "playing tennis". However, Sandy and I did win a doubles match in a school tournament at Jefferson. I cannot remember who our opponents were but we actually each won a small little trophy. We attributed our victory not to skill, but to our favorite lucky tennis balls which we named Bop-op and Shadda-lump-dump.

Coaches

Coach Smith was highly respected in Oak Ridge. She inspired us with her warm personality, her athletic abilities, and her enthusiasm. She coached the cheerleaders, led the pep rallies, and rode with us to away games on the Pep Bus. According to the 1959 Jefferson Eagle, Mrs. Smith "organized the cheering club. It met every Monday after school to practice yelling." 200 girls tried out for cheerleader that year. The faculty narrowed it down to 25 and the student body elected the final squad. Belated congratulations to our enthusiastic Jefferson cheerleaders: Barbie Henderson, Brenda McClendon, Sally Bainbridge, Cheryl Gambrel, Adrian Wilkinson, Candy Jones, Bama Rucker, Kathy Van Fleet, and Linda Aurin!

Coach Nick Orlando has left a legacy in Oak Ridge second to none. Stories of his paddle (it seemed to grow larger and stronger every year) put fear into many hearts, but at the same time, the boys bragged that signing it was a badge of honor. His raspy voice and booming laughter filled the halls, and he was very good at winning ball games. Even today football games at Jack Armstrong Stadium (Blankenship Field) continue to rely on the good luck phrase, "Will Coach Nick Orlando please report to the press box", but that's another story…

Over the Air

Radio station WATO (am) was a great source for local news and events, especially those of a social nature. Located near the bottom of East Drive, they broadcasted the ballgames, interviewed local celebrities and discussed current events, mostly related to Oak Ridge. We kids knew the DJs, and they took our song requests over the phone. We girls would sit for what seemed like hours dialing our princess phones, trying to get through. Sometimes we made up names and sometimes we were brave enough to use our real ones. I think the DJ's recognized our voices but they played along just the same. "Please dedicate," we would say, "Love Me Tender" from Josephine to Algernon." We were certain that only we "got" the secret meanings. It was our "social media" in the seventh grade.

He probably never even knew it, but I, along with most of my friends, had a crush on B.B. Bell. We knew his information by heart, "Burwell Baxter Bell, III, 104 Pickwick Lane, 5-3237. We would call his house, hoping he would answer the phone. He hardly ever did, but if he answered, we were too shy to speak to him, so we hung up.

There was no caller ID back then, so as far as we knew, our identities remained secret. My apologies to the Bell family for all those annoying calls back then. Little did we know that when we dedicated the song "Soldier Boy" to him, it was actually going out to the future Four-Star General B.B. Bell, commanding officer of the U.S. Army in Europe, then commanding officer of the U. S. Armed Forces in South Korea. Thank you, General Bell, from all your Oak Ridge friends and classmates for your distinguished service to our country.

Word of the Bird

Saturday afternoons during college football season, the radio at 108 Chatham Lane was always turned to WATO's "Scoreboard". Non-stop ball scores and updates, laced with familiar college fight songs, filled the house. It was another call-in show, and without computers, the announcers had quite a task, keeping up with scores being reported by phone from all around the country, and taking non-stop calls inquiring about a favorite team's status. Such excitement! Listeners anxiously awaited the Slippery Rock score, but I never quite knew why.

One Saturday morning, Oak Ridgers awoke to an unexpected blanket of snow. It was thick and icy, close to 10 inches deep. Roads were closed. Trapped at home, there was nothing to do but listen to the radio. The most popular song of the day was "Surfin' Bird" by The Trashmen. When the WATO staff finally made it in to work, the DJs came up with a novel idea. They would spin that 45 record, and as long as one more person would request it, they would continue playing that same song, over and over, and over. Out came the princess phones! I do not know how many times it played, but the marathon went on and on, all day long. If you remember the lyrics, you know what I'm talking about! Parents could not turn the radios off because they were needed for weather updates. We were a captive audience!

As it got close to time for "Football Scoreboard", Daddy started pacing. Wishing for snowshoes or skis, he threatened to sled down California and go break that 45 record. It wasn't necessary, probably because football fans were confiscating children's phones all over town. I think this Saturday has to go down in the official record books as The Secret City's most beautiful, yet annoying, day. Everybody's heard...about the bird...

Snow

That night, we got the sleds out. Roads remained closed, and the snow was beautiful, glistening in the moonlight. Neighbors began to gather at Clarion Road, up at the top of the ridge where California Avenue intersects with East and Outer Drives. We rode our sleds all the way down California, turning in at Chatham, and riding all the way down to the end of the Lane. It was kind of scary for me, and too much work to walk all the way back up for a second ride, but it was a once-in-a-lifetime event, none the less. Bobbie Smith even skied from her house on Outer Drive down California to the Oak Ridge Turnpike. She was awesome!

Even though we have a fairly mild climate, I remember a few more weather-related events in the 1960s. On January 10, 1962, I was in the ninth grade at Jefferson. Normally snows came overnight, with little or no warning. Often it snowed all around us, but not here in the valley (we were protected from extremes, just as Gen. Groves had predicted). This time, it was different; we awoke to twelve beautiful inches of fluffy white snow. About mid-day, the sun came out, but temperatures remained around ten degrees. I was certain we would be out of school all week. Certain, that is, until at 8:30 that night, WATO announced that despite a predicted temperature of five degrees, Oak Ridge Schools would open as usual on Thursday morning. Groan. Clinton City, closed; Anderson County, closed; Roane County, closed; Oak Ridge City Schools, OPEN. But on Thursday, January 11, a history-making day, word came out at 6 a.m.: No school in Oak Ridge.

The famous, dependable, ever-starting, always available buses would not start. Oak Ridge children were ecstatic! Actually, there were important reasons why our buses were always operational. First of course, was the temperate climate, even less extreme here, surrounded by the foothills. Second, these buses remained at the ready because they would be used in case of a necessary evacuation; and third, our roads were de-iced and cleared by crews specially trained by the federal government. Supplies were plentiful and a plan was always in effect to ensure that plant personnel could be on site as needed.

In addition, Oak Ridge students were required to be in class the maximum number of days allowed. Expectations were high, and the superintendent's job was to keep the schools open, no matter what. At one time the Secret City operated 600 buses. They always knew what to do.

At the Hop

We couldn't go to dances at the Wildcat Den until sophomore year at the high school, so sock hops often rocked the gym at Jefferson on Saturday nights. Coach Smith and Coach Orlando were always there to make sure all shoes were left at the door so no marks would scuff their perfectly polished gym floor. We kids would post lookouts at the top of the bleachers, looking out towards Kentucky Avenue. If someone was dancing without permission or talking to someone not on the parents' "approved list", or whatever secrets we wanted to keep just among us, "Parents on the Premises!" would alert us all, well in advance. Sometimes we had live bands and sometimes a DJ would play records. We didn't care, we just loved to dance. We were easily emotional, and do any of you admit that you still cry when you hear the song, "Teen Angel"?

The Harman Hudson

We ninth graders had our own personal after-school taxi service. So often we had club meetings or Student Council after class, or we stayed to decorate the gym for one of our dances, and we would miss the bus. Bill Harman drove over after high school in his green Hudson, picked up as many of us as we could cram into his car, and drove us home. It was up to us to organize and tell him whose house was next. It was easy; we just alphabetized ourselves! It was such fun, and Bill and his friend Vincent Webb remained our good friends all through high school. Looking back, I don't think we ever offered to pitch in on gas, and we probably should have, but it was never an issue. Gasoline cost only 28 cents per gallon back then, and we were all family, after all.

A boy named Sue

It wasn't easy, growing up as a girl named Clyde. Clyde Taliaferro Moore, to be exact. Even though I had a dear Aunt Clyde and my dad was Clyde (nicknamed Dorie) and my mother was Charlie (nicknamed Tot), I sometimes wished they had named me Claire. Claire Taliaferro (pronounced Tolliver) had such a nice ring to it, and life would have been much less complicated. Every year on the first day of school I would rush frantically through the halls to introduce myself to the teacher and beg him or her not to call me Clyde when the rolls were first read out loud. I really am a girl, I would tell them; PLEASE call me Tollie. As a rule, they honored my request, unless they forgot, but even in college it was embarrassing to raise my hand when the professor called out "Mr. Moore." It would have saved the Governor of Tennessee the job of sending me a letter my senior year. "Greetings," it began, "We hope you will consider a career in the United States Armed Forces, and please remember to register for the draft." Girls were excluded from the draft, and a career in the Armed Forces was definitely not in this girl's future plans! But I was, and still am, Clyde; friends and family often refer to me affectionately as Clyde, and people seldom forget my name! My parents' explanation for their name choice was "Oh, it was so stylish, back then, in the South." Yeah, Mom, me and a Boy Named Sue.

Oak Ridge High School

Sophomore year in the fall of 1962 was exciting and hectic as we decided what to wear, bought books, chose our elective classes, found our way through the long halls, learned how to work combination locks, signed up for sports and after school activities, met new friends from St. Mary's and Robertsville, reserved our tables in the cafeteria, and tried to figure out how to carry all those heavy books without dropping them. Advice from my parents was fairly simple. "You are known by the company you keep," they said; "Never behave in a manner which could deny you a government clearance. Do not gossip or betray a confidence. Remain strong in your faith, and remember, secrets are meant to be kept." Honor, respect, and reputation were important in our family. We had the Oak Ridge legacy to uphold, and pass on to future generations.

My uncle, Jack Maury, assistant ambassador to Greece, was also Chief of Station, CIA. So secret-keeping ran in the family. Cousin Cindy and I were invited to spend the following summer with them at the U. S. Embassy in Greece. Civil War was looming and the country became too dangerous so we didn't get to go, but that's another story...

Tollie Mayfield

In the early sixties, The Knoxville News Sentinel carried an "advice to the lovelorn"" column titled, "Ask Molly Mayfield." Since I was always interested in my friends' social affairs, and both willing and eager to offer advice, they nicknamed me "Tollie Mayfield." So it was only natural that when Pam Hemphill finished her term, I would inherit the title of the Oak Ridger's Teen Talk Topics columnist.

I wrote the column twice weekly from the spring of 1964 until graduation in 1965. The column was designed to highlight and report on various teenage activities as they occurred in Oak Ridge. I reported on everything from school events, club activities, dances and parties, church functions, concerts, awards, and contests, to who was dating whom, who attended certain events and the latest trends and fads, interspersed with my own opinions and comments. It was the closest we had to Facebook, back in the day.

Nancy McKay was my good friend and Swank-ette Sister. Her father, Don, was publisher of the Oak Ridger, and Dick Smyser was the editor. June Adamson was my boss and mentor. She seldom changed my copy unless she suspected a hidden meaning or maybe a coded message of some sort, which I admit I did try to sneak in from time to time. I was determined to be accurate. Reputations depended on it. Phone calls beginning with "Don't print my name this week. My parents don't know I was at that party..." or "be sure and put my name next to my boyfriend's..." were very common. Oh, the power of the printed word!

Kern Methodist

Beginning in 1951, my family and I attended Kern Memorial Methodist Church. Still located on Tennessee Avenue, it was a much smaller version of the church as it is today. I don't remember much about specific ministers as a young child but in 1959, Dr. Amos Rogers came to town. As our minister, he developed a very special relationship with the youth of Kern as well as others in the community. He was my spiritual advisor, my inspiration, and most of all, my friend.

Traditionally speaking, we Methodists like to sing, drink coffee, and make casseroles. Social times in the church were to me just as memorable as Sunday morning services. Our family usually sat near the back, on the right-hand side of the sanctuary. Mother's dear friend Virginia Boswell loved to slide into the pew behind us and whisper hilarious observations about various congregants as they entered the sanctuary around us, all dressed up in their hats, gloves, and "Sunday Best." It seems her primary motivation was to make Mother and me giggle in church. It was all in good fun. She never missed a Sunday, and I loved her like family.

In the early years, as the holidays approached, the Kern Men's Club sold Christmas trees in the church parking lot. Sometimes Daddy would take me with him and on cold nights, they would build a big bonfire, right on the black-top. They tossed in evergreens, and the whole neighborhood smelled like Christmas. The women served us homemade cookies, apples, and hot chocolate with marshmallows. Music and laughter filled the air, and there was pride in knowing that profits were going to a good cause, especially at that time of year.

As we became teenagers, Dr. Rogers brought in youth mission groups from all around the world for city-wide participation. He made sure our activities were current and relevant, and he challenged us both spiritually and intellectually. I still carry the Bible given to me at confirmation.

I was active in the youth choir, Sunday school, and MYF (Methodist Youth Fellowship). I hear there is a story floating around about me, Dewey Ewing, and Dottie Foster, hanging out in the parking lot after MYF, but since I don't remember the details, I had best leave the telling to them. We did have fun at Kern!

Methodist Youth Camp was held each year at Big Ridge, homeland of the famous Ranger Robb. One year, our high schoolers were serving as junior counselors. On the night before the last day of camp, sitting out on the pier talking and telling jokes (with permission), at 2:30 a.m., a little voice came out of the dark: "Kids, kids, this is the ranger." Assuming someone was playing a trick, the "kids" of course replied, "Ranger, ranger, this is the kids!" No trick, it was our own Ranger Sam. He announced that he had strict orders to "send anyone under age 18 caught on the pier after dark directly to jail." He then proceeded to line everyone up, single file, with instructions to "keep all hands where I can see them." The long march to Ranger Robb's office was at least a quarter of a mile. Ranger Sam really thought he had a catch, but as usual at Big Ridge, Ranger Robb saved the day, and provided yet another happy ending to a week at Big Ridge State Park.

But then there was "Daddy D". Many of my friends went to St. Stephens Episcopal Church, and many friends from other denominations attended their youth program as well. The leader was Father Daniels, a handsome, cool, hip, charismatic young priest, affectionately known as "Daddy D". Although I was tempted, and occasionally attended events with my friends, my ties to Kern were strong and I remained loyal.

Dr. Rogers died tragically at a young age, leaving a hole in the soul of our city that can never be refilled. Today, Sundays find Michael and me back in those same pews, continuing the Kern tradition...

Glow Sticks

Ridges surrounding the Secret City are composed of mostly oak trees, sprinkled in the spring with blossoming redbuds and dogwoods, and blazing into beautiful golden colors in the fall. Breath-taking views from atop these ridges rotate like a kaleidoscope as the seasons change. This spot was chosen, we are told, as the least likely in the country to have earthquakes, floods, tornadoes, or any other extreme weather. Initially important from a scientific point of view, it has proved to be an accurate assessment, and a wonderful place for raising families. It wasn't, however, and sometimes still isn't, such a great place for television reception!

People have asked me, through the years, if it was scary, growing up here. To some it probably seemed so, but we were watched and protected more than most, living in the shadow of a national nuclear reservation. The general consensus was that if those who worked in and managed these facilities also chose to live here with their families, we were happy to live here as well. As the Cold War continued to grow colder, Oak Ridge was said to be Number Seven on the enemy's target list. That was something to be concerned about, but as a young person I reasoned that since we were not on any maps, most likely the enemy could never find us anyway.

As the Oak Ridge story became more available to the public, there were questions about things like radioactivity in the air and pollution in the water, and was it safe to fish the streams. I trusted our scientists to have the study well in hand, and they have done so as issues have developed through the years. It is only natural that questions would arise regarding life in a nuclear Secret City. When microwave ovens came along, we definitely did not refer to them as "nuking it", and I did not glow in the dark!

Safety Nets

Della and Floyd Culler lived with their son Jimmy in an F house down at the end of Oneida Lane. Floyd was head of the Nuclear Division at Oak Ridge National Laboratory. Like Nick Antonas at Y-12 today, Floyd was a dedicated professional who genuinely cared about the well-being of all his Oak Ridge workers and their families. He and Della were just as comfortable sipping cocktails in our living room as they were at a large social gala in Washington, D.C. They, along with others like Harriet and Sam Bolt, Larry and Lib Corbin, Jeanie and Bill Wilcox, Dru and Pete Mazur, and the Dunnigans, were family friends. They seemed to me like a giant unspoken umbrella, shielding, sheltering, and supporting us, ever-watchful and always there if needed. So yes, America, we did feel safe.

Oak Ridge Country Club

I spent a lot of time at the Oak Ridge Golf and Country Club. The club's slogan was "Good Golfing…With Scenic Splendor." Golf pro "Rabbit" Grove provided a great

Junior Golf Program. There were youth tournaments through the years, always ending with patio parties and trophy presentation ceremonies. One year I won first place in the girls' division in the Under 12 age group. It was a 5-hole tournament. Robert Walker won the boys' division with a 34 and I shot 32. However, my small trophy paled in comparison to my friend Mandy's larger one, and I was jealous. She was a year younger than I was, and she won first prize for the largest number of putts!

Golf carts were seldom used by anyone back then. Caddies were available, but usually everyone just walked. I loved golf, but I dreaded trudging up the number nine fairway in the heat. Salt tablets were taken but did no good and all I could think about was how great it would feel to finally jump into the pool. Judy Lane was by far the best golfer in our crowd. She could drive the green on the third hole with her putter. In 1964 Terry Barker was Junior Champion and Mary DePersio won the girls' division. Fred Von der Lage, Judy, and Tommy DePersio, among others, were Junior Champions as well.

In addition to parties and dances, there were family fish fries every Friday night in the summer. Sometimes the pool hours were extended until 11:00 and we loved swimming under the stars. Children were not allowed in the 19th Hole but the grown-ups sure seemed to have a lot of fun in there. Ladies played golf during the day and the men played later, after work. Everyone played on weekends.

One Saturday my mother and Della Culler were putting on Number Eight green, when a snake wriggled out of the high grass and slithered toward them. They dropped their clubs and ran screaming up the Number Ten fairway towards the club house, certain that the giant copperhead was in hot pursuit. Dad and Floyd, preparing to tee off at Number Ten, heard them coming. They hijacked Rabbit's golf cart and like Poppy Ott and the Giant Snake Hunters, set off to save the day. They retrieved the ladies' clubs and bags and finally returned to the Clubhouse, assuring everyone that Hole Number Eight was once again safe, and play could resume. Mom and Della spent the rest of the day in the Nineteenth Hole!

Through the years, lots of celebrities and dignitaries, including world leaders and their wives, have played on the links at the Oak Ridge Country Club. They were often necessarily incognito, yet it is easy to imagine that many important plans and decisions have been worked out and firmed up on these fairways and greens. These official, often clandestine, visits would as a rule have been kept secret, but it was a star-studded event a few years later when Arnold Palmer and Mason Rudolph came to town.

Today the beautiful trees surrounding the course have grown taller and denser, making the entire area even more breath-takingly beautiful. I find it a little sad that people today have so much less leisure time and families don't gather here as much as we used to. However, good golfing and scenic splendor still abound in and around the Secret City. Keyes Fillauer's annual charity golf tournament has become a wonderful Oak Ridge tradition, but that's another story…

The Upside-Down Acorn

We, the second generation, were raised in an era of enthusiastic optimism. We entered Oak Ridge High School well prepared and looking forward to a bright and safe future in a new world of freedom and opportunity. We were not wealthy, but we were richly endowed. During these years, our high school campus was renovated. Construction included adding two new modern circular brick buildings, along with other upgrades and improvements. We listened to the noise of the trucks and bulldozers and were reminded of that first graduating class who were studying here under similar yet much harder conditions. We were getting a state-of-the-art facility for 1800 students. They were getting a basic building for 50 special students who had left everything behind to come with their parents to help win World War II. We honor them.

I don't know who first discovered the upside-down acorn. The bright white symbol of the atom with an acorn at its center was a gift from us, the class of 1965. It stands out against the brick cafeteria wall, clearly visible from Oak Ridge Turnpike. The acorn and the atom seemed a fitting combination to symbolize our vision of the city. Our class motto was, "To look backward with pride, to look forward with hope," from Robert Frost's poem, "The Death of the Hired Man." I don't know when it was finally corrected, but sometime after we graduated, the symbol was re-installed, this time with the acorn right-side-up!

The Wildcat Den

One of the best things about making it to tenth grade and entering Oak Ridge High School was getting a Den Card. Located in an original government building (Mid-town Center today) the Wildcat Den was the social center of our high school universe. Operated by the city recreation department, it was a youth center for ORHS students only.

There were weekend dances with live bands, and dances held just for us on summer nights after hours at the Oak Ridge Swimming Pool. It served as a teenage hangout after school and on Saturdays, with pool tables, ping pong, card games, a juke box, and so forth.

Friday nights after ball games we would head to the Wildcat Den and dance for hours. Shep Lauter was the man in charge and he did a great job. He had his hands full, keeping an eye on things. Sometimes there were 600 kids dancing inside, and more turned away at the door. No one was allowed in without a current Den card; no one from Clinton, no college students, and not even parents unless absolutely necessary. Admission was free, thanks to the City Recreation Department, which picked up the tab. Sometimes Shep would accompany boys to the parking lot to inspect the trunks of their cars. If he found any unapproved beverages, he would generally deal with it himself, and the usual suspects were carefully monitored. Loitering outside was not allowed. Packed in like sardines, it was hard to cause trouble. We came to dance, and dance we did!

Shep Lauter was an outstanding man. A great role model, he was loved and respected by Oak Ridge citizens of all ages. There were over 1800 students in the three grades at ORHS in the 1964-65 school year. The Wildcat Den building was originally designed to hold 200. We were bursting at the seams.

It all started with a Teen Talk Topics column in the Oak Ridger. I was really concerned about the overcrowding problem. The Den was intended for all students, not just those who could arrive first. After the ballgames, players had to shower and such and although the dance was a celebration in honor of the team, they often arrived late, and were turned away. Shep hated this most of all. It was hot and crowded, and becoming much less fun than it should be. The fire marshal was on the verge of shutting us down.

I began writing columns and stirring up interest in finding a solution. As managing editor of our school newspaper, The Oak Leaf, and with the publicity help of my friend and editor-in-chief, Bonnie Holz, I spearheaded a campaign. We formed a Student Council committee, with the help of our faculty sponsor, Mr. Jules Crocker, to discuss feelings, suggestions and ideas, which were pouring in from around the community.

It evolved into a committee of 13 adults and six students, two from each class, and others elected as needed. These members were Mr. and Mrs. Raymond Stripling, Mr. and Mrs. Al Faloon, Mr. and Mrs. B.B. Bell, Jr., Mr. and Mrs. Claude Workman, Jr., Mr. and Mrs. Ted Kwasnoski, Mr. and Mrs. Clyde Moore, and Mr. Bill Unger, along with school advisor Mr. Crocker. Teenage members were Pam Lofton, Macky McMahon, Robbie Unger, Peggy Snyder, Danny Schimmel, Butch DeBord, and myself.

I contacted the local National Guard Armory and they were willing to let us use their facility on the Turnpike for dances until something permanent could be arranged. Our efforts grew, and the Youth Center Action Committee (YCAC) was formed. A feasibility study was completed and with the total support of city recreation director Carl Yearwood, City Council voted to move forward with the project, and plans for the new Youth Center as part of a larger complex were underway. I graduated and went off to college, confident that our plan was in good hands and our goals were being met.

Located near the downtown shopping area and across the Oak Ridge Turnpike from our high school, the Oak Ridge Civic Center today is a multi-million dollar facility, including a public library, indoor swimming pool, youth center, indoor sports facility, small meeting rooms, an auditorium, fountain square, large outdoor amphitheater, walking track, playground, Bissell Memorial Park, and the Peace Bell. Today, as a senior citizen living in the Secret City, I look proudly at this fabulous facility, and remember fondly what we high school students accomplished, so many years ago.

Baby Blue

One Saturday morning Daddy announced that we needed a new car. He was going down to Cleveland to see his good friend Bobby Card who owned a car dealership. He said we needed a good, dependable, sturdy, family station wagon. As a teenager, I dreaded what it would look like and wondered if I would ever even dare to be seen in it, much less drive it to high school.
Eleven-year-old Cutch pointed out that at least it could carry a whole lot of my friends and we could pile a whole lot of stuff into it, and if we went camping (we never did), we could put the back seat down and make it into a bed. I could not be consoled, and Mother didn't even try. Moping around in my Swank-ette purple bedroom, I finally heard Cutch say, "He's here!" We rushed outside and there was Daddy, standing proudly beside our beautiful new powder-blue Ford Galaxie 500 convertible. This time I was still inconsolable, choked up with happy tears.

Cars

Once we started driving, there were strict curfews; not imposed by the city, but by our parents. Yet still, we had more than our share of fun. Maybe we got a little rowdy but we were rule-followers for the most part. We learned how to roll back the odometer on Jackie Seagull's car so our occasional unreported trips to Knoxville could go undetected. A little mischief once in a while kept life interesting. My mother once said that if I was to be home at 11:00 and I estimated being home at 11:10, I would stop somewhere and call. There was no phone in the bedroom, so someone had to get up and go answer the one that was tethered to the wall in the kitchen. By the time she got back to bed, I was already home! I guess it was a little excessive, but I valued my ungrounded freedom, and I liked to be accurate.

The Skyway Drive-in movie theater was one of the largest in the country. Built in 1944 at 480 Old Highway 62 (where the Kroger parking lot off Illinois Avenue is today), there were speakers for 500 cars, and the screen was gigantic. Typical drive-ins in the day would accommodate an average of maybe two or three hundred vehicles. It was a popular hangout on hot summer nights and sometimes they would offer "one price per car" specials. We would pack in as many bodies as we could, sort of like stuffing a phone booth. What we neglected to mention was that sometimes the trunk would also be packed full of bodies! Once we parked, the stowaways would sneak out and spend the evening in the chairs down front or socializing from car to car. We made sure to buy popcorn, and it usually wasn't about the movie anyway.

ORHS Teachers

The teaching staff at Oak Ridge High School really was exceptional. Mr. Dale Woodiel, head of the English and journalism departments, served as advisor for The Oak Leaf (newspaper), the Oak Log (annual), and The Other Road (literary magazine). He also sponsored the journalism honor society, Quill and Scroll. New to Oak Ridge, he had a more liberal point of view than most of the staff. He taught us critical thinking, creativity, and integrity. He often reminded us that freedom and responsibility should always go hand in hand. We were fortunate to have him senior year as he was awarded a John Hay Fellowship and would take a sabbatical the following year to study the humanities at Harvard. One of the highlights of our Senior Prom was watching Mr. Woodiel dance the Watusi with fellow teacher Miss Smith!

Mr. Lipscomb taught us Algebra II. He was always amused when I fell for Lyn Trapp's pencil trick, over and over and over again. My friend Lynn, a senior, talked about fixing me up with some of his friends on the football team, but instead, he just kept coming back to that same old phrase, "still too young." Well, Lynn, now I am 66 years old, but in reality, I think I am probably still too young!

Miss Margaret Gottshall was my physical education teacher. She taught us to play field hockey. It was the only team sport I ever participated in, and I really liked it. Our field was located on the Turnpike side of the campus, where the tennis courts are today. My only problem was that in order to reach the field, we had to cross over the creek, and in order to cross the creek, we had to balance along a big cedar log. I was just certain that if anyone was going to fall into that creek, it would be me. I just didn't trust my slick-soled white Keds gym shoes. Once across, the field hockey was fun, but I dreaded the return trip. I was often late to the showers because I was the last one, and the slowest one, to cross THE LOG. Miss Gottshall never penalized me for being late. We never talked about it, but I knew she understood. She was a first-class teacher and I learned a lot more from Miss Gottshall than just my field hockey skills.

Miss Ruth Frazier taught World History. She also taught my dad at Bradley County High School in Cleveland, before she moved to Oak Ridge, so he was very sympathetic when I was kept up late at night studying for her tough exams. She insisted that we call it "Sah-oo-die Arabia, and her wise worldly predictions continue to come true in our modern world today.

Mrs. Martine Borie, Mrs. Sylvia Countess, and Mrs. Dora Davidson taught me three solid years of French. They instilled in me a true love of the language and by the time I entered college, I was practically fluent. The Thibaut family in our textbooks became like our own family. We all memorized the following verses from French I, and I still remember them today. They might just remain familiar to many of you as well:

> J'entre dans la salle de classe.
> Je regarde autour de moi.
> Je vois les eleves et le professeur.
> Je dis bonjour au professeur.
> Je prends ma place.

There were two Miss Turners on the high school staff in 1962. Masal Turner, hired 20 years earlier by Dr. Blankenship, practically invented the English language. She could hear a mis-used pronoun or a double negative from halfway down the hall, and she never hesitated to make a public example of it. Masal turner was both feared and revered.

Lucy T

Lucille Turner taught Latin II. She was also a long-time ORHS teacher. She knew just about all there was to know about the ancient Romans and their language. "Amo, amas, amat. Amamos, amatis, amant" is etched forever in my brain. Miss Turner stood barely five feet tall. She looked like a little dill pickle, with lines and bumps and a tight little gray bun perched on top of her head. She was very dedicated to our education. She was also very naïve, and she waddled.

Escapades in her class were hilarious. She routinely gave us "pop" quizzes, usually on Mondays, comprised of 10 multiple choice questions, two of which were repeats from the week before, just for review. She kept a clipboard with her at all times, upon which the day's lesson plan or "pop" quiz, along with the answers, was prominently displayed in nice large print. Every week like clockwork, one of the taller boys would go up to her and, putting an arm around her shoulders, tell her how nice she looked today, and in his best Eddie Haskell voice, continue to flatter and talk nonsense, while another boy would slip up behind them and read all ten answers to the questions, relaying them to the class via sign language. Flattery got us everywhere. She fell for it every time, basking in the complimentary glow.

Often someone would misbehave on purpose by, for example, throwing a paper airplane. He would immediately be banished to the desk she had placed by the door out in the hallway, for just such occasions. From there he became the lookout, and mischief would ensue. The boys knew exactly how long it took her to waddle down to the principal's office. They had her timed exactly, round trip. Someone would go to the restroom and return, telling Miss Turner that she (Miss Turner) needed to go to the office, immediately. Making it sound as if she were being summoned, it really meant that she needed to go to the office because WE needed her to go. The plan always worked.

Once while she was waddling her way down to the office, all of our desks got piled into the back of the classroom, out of sight behind the large petition. When she came back, there we sat in our chairs, behind our invisible desks. We all began talking at once, bemoaning our lost desks and wondering frantically, what should we do, and how could we ever get along without them? Once again, concerned, baffled, and perplexed, off she waddled to the office to report the missing desks. When she returned, this time accompanied by the principal, there we sat like innocent little statues, books opened atop our seemingly undisturbed desks, and smiling sweetly as we awaited her return.

Another time, upon returning from another goose chase (goose waddle) to the office, she found us all wandering about the room, frantically looking for a missing classmate. Boys were looking under desks, opening drawers, and checking behind the window curtains. He was nowhere to be found. Finally, a voice from over by the second floor window hollered out, "I've got him, Miss Turner!" She waddled on over to the finder, who was stretching both his arms out the open window. He held one shoe in each hand, soles facing upward, and just as she got close, he held up the empty shoes, sighing, "oops." "Quick, Miss Turner," we all began yelling, "You better go get him!" Before she could make it out the door, in came the missing classmate, looking a little disheveled, but able to muster a whisper, "Whew, ...I'm all right." We were naturally relieved, as the bell was about to ring, and we now had an extra night to study for the big Latin test.

It was always easy to distract Miss Turner and get her off track. Someone would ask a silly question like, "Miss Turner, do you think Antony really loved Cleopatra or was he just after her money?" or "Did Brutus really kill Julius Caesar or could it maybe have been some kind of mafia hit?" or "What is an Ide? Were they only in March and why do we have to beware them anyway?" And then, of course we would all join in, exclaiming how interesting the question was, and how we really needed to know the answer, offering our thoughts and comments on the subjects, and talking all at once. By the time order was restored, there wasn't enough time left to take the test!

Sometimes after a large test someone would tell Miss Turner that we really knew how hard she worked for us and maybe she needed a break from grading all those papers. We would be glad to pitch in and help. We could just exchange test papers among ourselves and grade each others', saving her all that time and effort. Without waiting for her answer, mass confusion took over. Test papers and students began shuffling back and forth and up and down. Somehow out of that chaos came test papers, returned to owners, properly graded and corrected, and mostly marked with A's. She was so proud of how well we were learning Latin. Now don't get me wrong. It sort of seems like cheating, but the fact is, we really did know our Latin. We were probably just bored. Latin II was one of my all-time favorite classes, and we honestly took our mid-terms and final exams very seriously. I don't know who thought up all these shenanigans, but if anyone wants to come forward and claim credit, I'm all ears. You know who you are. And besides, I bet there is a classroom roster somewhere, back in the high school archives...

Social Clubs

Girls' Social Clubs were important at Oak Ridge High School in the 1960's. Traditions change with the years, and today they could not play the same part in modern high school culture. But times were different back then and they were recognized as socially acceptable both by the school and the community. Highly organized with constitutions and by-laws, the clubs were not only social, they were actively involved with civic and charity work as well.

The three girls' clubs were Penguins, Sub-Debs, and Swank-ettes. There were also two boys' clubs, The Gents and the Chanticleers. Each club had their own distinctive car honk. The Penguin Honk was Dot-dit-dot-dit-dot-dot-dot (Here's to Penguins, We're True Blue); Sub-Debs, dot-dot-dot (Sub-Deb Love)and Swank-ettes, dit-dit-dot (Swak-ette Love). I never really knew what the boys' official honks were. They just liked to make a lot of noise! These car honks floated all over town. Sometimes girls announced themselves every time they drove by a friend's house, and sometimes they honked the friend's honk also. If several girls were in the car, the stream of honks could go on for hours!

Every August, just before school started in the fall, the girls hosted a big Inter-club rush party on a Saturday night at the Oak Ridge swimming pool. Beautiful after dark, it was decorated with candles and flowers and a delicious buffet was set up on long tables by the water. Invitations were sent out to all rising sophomore girls and everyone was encouraged to attend.

Representatives from each club gave welcoming speeches, told about their clubs and explained what to expect during rush week. Dressed up in fancy island costumes, club members mingled with guests throughout the evening as many special memories and lasting friendships were formed. Sophomore girls then spent the next several weeks trying to decided which, if any, sorority best suited their needs, and in return, the clubs were deciding which girls they would be inviting to join.

Rush Parties and Silent Week

Individual clubs had their own rush parties. I remember going out to Sonja Wilde's house for a barn party and hayride. She lived in the big white house across Melton Hill Lake and it was an elaborate Swank-ette affair, with costumes, horseback rides, a campfire and wonderful food. Another year we decorated Janet and Lynn Stoner's house on Outer Drive as the S. S. Swank-ette , for a "Showboat" rush slumber party. The "Down South" Players presented a melodrama, "Sweet Swank-ette Sue". The cast included Brenda McClendon as Sue, Jackie Seagull as the ever-evil villain, Snydley Whiplash, Sarah Fritts as Sue's dirt-diggin' daddy, and Marilyn Ripley as her brother Ringo, yeah, yeah, yeah. Super heroes who saved the day were Sue Swartout as Superman, Sarah Sensenbach as Mighty Mouse, Lynn Whittaker as Rocky the Squirrel, and Linnhe Kopplin as Dudley Do-Wrong. I have no memory of the plot, if there was one, but it was a grand production, just the same!

The week between rush parties and pledge night was called Silent Week. Inter-club rules required that no club member could speak to, be in a car with, or associate in any way with any sophomore girl, even during school. Finally at the end of Silent Week, after much anticipation, the long-awaited pledge night arrived. I really wanted to join The Swank-ette Social Club. I felt a true connection to so many of the members and it just always seemed like the natural choice for me to make. My friends and family all concurred, but of course in the end, it was not my choice to make, but theirs.

Swank-ettes

I was pledged by Sub-Debs and Penguins, and I held my breath, hoping that the Swank-ettes would also come to my house. At last I heard them, cars honking as they made their way up California Avenue. The honks grew louder as they approached Chatham Lane, but instead of turning in, they passed by, and Swank-ette horns grew silent. Maybe they are going on up to Brenda McClendon's house first, and then come back down the hill, I thought. Something was terribly wrong. I told Mom to just turn off the porch light, they weren't coming. I was so sad.

Little did I know, they were teasing me and my parents were in on it. They sneaked down the lane, at least 20 cars, all full of Swank-ettes, headlights turned off. Suddenly there was a knock at the door. I didn't want to answer. Daddy finally convinced me to turn on the porch light and open up the door. I did, and there they were, my future Swank-ette sisters, all singing to me:

Swank-ettes, Swank-ettes
Good and true,
Come tonight to ask of you
Tollie, Tollie, here's to you,
Won't you come along and be a Swank-ette too!
Got along without you, before we met you,
Couldn't get along without you now...

What seemed like hundreds of hugs and thousands of happy tears filled the night. I still don't know whose idea it was, but thanks to my good friend Pattie Corbin, it was truly a night to remember.

I accepted immediately, and it wasn't until the next day that I got the news. One of our group had not been pledged by Swank-ettes, so everyone was going Penguin. Things might have been different if I had known, but I stayed true to my commitment. It worked out well for me. My dearest friends stayed as close as ever, and I cherished my new friends in Swank-ettes. Anne's parents didn't let her join a club, so she was our perfect liaison. I got a sweet note from Penguin senior Susan Yearwood, saying she was disappointed I hadn't chosen to be a Penguin, but she admired me for following my heart and honoring my word. She knew I would become a great Swank-ette sister. She was so gracious, and her message meant the world to me.

Pledge Week

Pledge week was a little scary for sophomores, fun for juniors, empowering for seniors, and very entertaining for others looking on. Our principal, Mr. Thomas Dunnigan, was patient and kind, but he established firm boundaries which we were required to honor. Staff was fully aware of the goings-on, and as far as I know we got through it without any major confrontations. It must have been hard for teachers to hide their amusement, and "business as usual" inside the classroom was quite a challenge. These activities had been part of the high school tradition for many, many years, so they knew just what was going on, and how to make the best of it.

Beginning Sunday night of Pledge Week, a few club members went to each pledge's home each evening, and with the help of the parents, chose "lovely" outfits to be worn to school the next day. Pledges were not allowed to wash their hair. Bright red lipstick highlighted the make-up of choice, and could be ordered re-applied, throughout the day. Mis-matched shoes and socks were in order and my big sister brought me special jewelry. It was a giant white raw onion, peeled and threaded on purple yarn, to be worn around my neck at all times, for the whole week. Whenever I received her command, I had to take a bite of it. Grimaces were frowned upon. Thanks a lot, Margie Garrigan!

We pledges were given all kinds of assignments. I had to find out all of senior football star Ray Armstrong's clothes sizes, including underwear. The girls didn't realize that his younger brother Ralph was my good buddy, so I had an easy time with that task. Seniors were always right. We carried their books and cafeteria trays. We opened doors, we bowed, and we "yes, ma'amed" our way all through the long week. But it was worth it, and I couldn't wait to become a senior so I could take revenge and humiliate the lowly sophomore pledges. According to my Swank-ette little sisters, Mary Helen Bender and Pam Cloyd, I was mean, and I did a really good job of acting my part!

Pledge week ended with an initiation ceremony. Ours was held at Karen Hildebrand's home. We labeled it our "night of horror", but it was probably pretty mild by today's standards. We became acquainted with eggs, flour, and minnows. We lamented the fate of poor Dewbie, as we performed our 1960's version of a rap, Rock-ettes style:

> 'Twas a dark and stormy night,
> When my Dewbie went away-eeeee.
> Never will forget it 'til my dyin' day.
> She was Sweet Sixteen, the Village Queen.
> Purtiest little thang that ye ever did see...
> Thangs ain't been the same
> Since my Dewbie went away.
> Roosters won't crow and the hens won't lay...

Does anyone remember the rest of the words?

We continued with pre-assigned skits until 3 a.m., when we were returned home to our nice warm beds. Then, two hours later, at 5 a.m. Saturday morning, we were dragged back to Karen's house to clean up the mess. It wasn't easy, but we didn't care. We had made it through, and we were finally Swank-ette Sisters. My Penguin friends are yet to reveal the recipe for initiation Penguin Stew. I know we keep our secrets well, but come on girls, it's been 50 years!

Swank-ette Sisters

Installation was held at the home of our president, Carol Ann Rothermel. It was a Sunday afternoon tea, and we dressed up in our nicest dresses, heels, and white gloves. The candle-light ceremony was very moving, as we solemnly promised to honor the standards of our club with both our attitude and behavior. We were given beautiful purple and white corsages and we sang our club song, "Deep Purple." In the final ceremony, each big sister pinned her new little sister with a sterling silver top hat and cane, which we wore proudly, every day. Our slogan was "Swank-ettes Forever," and I am sure that we are all still sisters, even though we seldom see each other these days. It's another family, Secret City style.

Barbara Martin was elected Swank-ette president our senior year. I gave her a good run for the money but when the votes were tallied, she clearly won, and I was happy to be her vice-president. Barbara's family owned Martin Funeral Home on the Turnpike, and the family living quarters were on the upstairs level. Mrs. Martin was our Swank-ette Mother. Club meetings were held once a week and were generally pretty routine, consisting of a business meeting, a short social time, and refreshments. Dues were fifty cents per week.

One particular night was anything but routine. Meeting at Barbara's house, we were instructed to park in the back, go up to the top of the stairs, and open the door on the right. We got most of it right, only instead of opening the door on the right, we opened the one on the left. The room was dimly lit, but it only took a minute for us to realize it was the embalming room, and there was a body on the table!!! We screamed, as only a crowd of teenage girls can, scampering back down the narrow steps, and out the door. Barbara came running down to see what all the ruckus was about, and there we were, a big clump of her Swank-ette sisters, huddled in the parking lot, hysterical. Libby and Louise Johnson were white as sheets. Joyce Freels' pretty blue eyes were big as saucers, and Brenda Brown kept insisting, over and over again that she would never go up those stairs again, EVER. Mrs. Martin soon came down, and gracious as always, insisted we come back upstairs, only quietly this time, as there was a funeral in progress downstairs. Barbara calmly led the way back up the steps, and we had our meeting, guaranteed to go down in the Swank-ette archives as one we would never forget.

Club Dances

As I have mentioned before, we Second Generationers loved our dances. Each of the three social clubs hosted one big formal affair each year, to which all were invited. Tickets were usually three dollars, and they were held in special venues, usually in Knoxville. We wore long gloves with our long formal gowns. Corsages and boutonnieres were specially designed to co-ordinate perfectly with our outfits.

My mother worked at Price Florist on the Oak Ridge Turnpike during those years and she loved taking the calls and talking to the boys about just what flowers to choose. She felt that carnations and roses were fine for sophomores but gardenias and orchids should wait for senior year. She knew who was taking whom to the dance and I couldn't wait for her to come home and tell me all the news. Since she knew so many of us girls, she didn't mind calling for descriptions of dresses, and to make sure whether or not a wrist corsage was needed. It was hard to pin a big corsage to a strapless gown!

Details completed, she then passed the orders on to Mrs. Hazel Price, floral designer extraordinaire, and between them they got it right, and hundreds of corsages were alphabetized in the cooler and ready to be picked up. On Saturday morning the boys arrived in droves. They lined up almost down to the Turnpike and cars overflowed into the Martin Funeral Home parking lot next door. The girls had to pick up boutonnieres for their dates as well. However, since many of us were home getting ready, with our hair rolled up in "dippity do" and orange can curlers, a parent usually took over that duty.

Club members decorated extensively for these dances. They were formal events with engraved invitations. Each dance centered around a special theme and formal pictures captured the moment as couples posed in front of a fancy backdrop. Couples were given engraved napkins and specially designed dance programs as souvenirs. Senior year our theme was "Bourbon Street" and it was held in Knoxville at the Kerbella Temple.

Maurice Williams and the Zodiacs, who had a number one song entitled "Stay", played "on Bourbon Street" as Swank-ettes and their escorts were presented out of the Silver Slipper night club, along a red carpet. Senior members were each presented with a bouquet of long-stemmed white roses by flower bearers, Joan Freels and Donnie Sanders. Tables were decorated with large dice and hands of cards and the ceiling was done in silver and gold. After the presentation ceremony, the girls sang "Let us call you Sweetheart" to club sweeties Joe and Jerry Harmon, and the band played "Deep Purple" in a special dance for Swank-ettes and their dates. My parents were among the chaperones. When they realized what fun we were having, they all pitched in and gave the band an extra $50.00 and they played another hour. Thank you, Ethel Howell. We knew just what to do!

Charity Work

Even though they were called social clubs, we also did a lot of charity work and community service. In honor of President Kennedy's birthday, we raised money for his library and we held bake sales to help support the Mental Health Center. We were Altrusa Girls and ORCMA belles and we ushered and sold tickets to the Oak Ridge Playhouse. At Christmas we went caroling around town with other organizations, raising money for Recording for the Blind. Many Saturday mornings were spent selling Krispy-Kreme donuts. Neighborhood lawnmowers would suddenly become silent at the sight of purple sweatshirts carrying stacks of white and green boxes, walking down the street!

Pam

Pamela Addison holds a special place in my heart. Pam was a treasured Swank-ette sister, and Pam had cancer. Her father was Captain Artie Addison, a well-respected member of the Oak Ridge Police Department. He and Mrs. Addison were determined that Pam should live her life to the fullest and I like to think that we, her friends, helped to achieve that goal. Her cancer grew worse, but she was still active, even when her leg was amputated. Pam died sophomore year and we, her Swank-ette sisters were honorary pall bearers. Our city mourned together and for many of us teenagers it was our first experience with death. We were well cared-for by school staff, churches and our extended family, the City of Oak Ridge. Pam's parents

118

became our "Swank-ette parents". In a way, Captain Addison comforted us through the years by helping to keep our city safe, and so it was only fitting that we comfort them in return.

Hangouts

The Snow White Diner on the Turnpike and the Mayflower Grill in Jackson Square are legendary Oak Ridge restaurants, but our crowd's favorites were the Blue Circle and the Brown Cow. The Blue Circle was similar to Krystal, but instead of a drive-by window, we parked and honked our horn to order food. Circling the Circle was a favorite activity and there was a pole on one side which made a tight squeeze for the circling cars. The pole was decorated with "battle scars": multicolored streaks of car paint. It was considered an honor if your color was there, and I must admit, there was a small streak of powder- blue. After the standard order of cheeseburger, fries, and homemade cherry pie, it was one more circle 'round, and a honk to say thank-you, delicious as usual.

Across the side street and next to Martin Funeral Home was the Brown Cow Drive-In. They charged fifty cents for a cup of homemade vanilla ice cream, and five cents more for a dollop of chopped walnuts drenched in ooey gooey homemade caramel syrup. It was practically impossible to drive by after school without stopping in for that special treat, the famous "Nickel Nuts."

Shoney's

Social life in The Ridge changed dramatically when Shoney's came to town. There was curb service. You could park, order, and eat in your car, or as in most cases for us second generationers, park and socialize. When we first saw the big 18-wheeler pull into the back parking lot, life as we knew it was changing. Strawberries, as big as apples, it seemed! Barney (not his name, but we called him that in honor of Barney Fife on the Andy Griffith Show) was Shoney's official security guard. He claimed to carry a gun, but no one ever saw it. In our minds, real armed security guards worked at places like Y-12, X-10, and K-25, not at restaurants; but we played along, and pretended to be scared. There were lots of rules, according to Barney. Barney's Rules of Order. You could only circle the restaurant three times without buying food. He was counting. Of course we just went somewhere else for a few minutes and then came back and drove around some more. You could not switch cars. If you arrived in one vehicle, you were not allowed to swap seats with a friend and depart in a different vehicle. We had to be careful. Barney was keeping track. There would be no loitering, and no sitting on trunks or hoods of cars in order to engage in group conversations, meaningful or otherwise. This could be dangerous.

Fortunate was I to drive a convertible! Seatbelts were not required, so we could pile in a crowd, drive around, honk our club honks over and over, and talk to friends in multiple cars, all at the same time. This was a complex issue for Barney, but a few well-chosen complimentary words usually calmed him down.

It's not as if we didn't spend a lot of money at Shoney's. Whenever any of us girls had a problem requiring "group talk", we would gather at a table inside and drown our sorrows in Big Boys, onion rings, and strawberry pie. No matter what was going on in our often dramatic social circle, things were always better after Shoney's. These sessions evolved and soon we discovered the magic of Hot Fudge Cake!

Barney also had food rules. There would be no sharing. If you ordered a sandwich, no one else could have a bite. French fries were private, and so was ketchup. Don't even think about sharing a Coke. He was the health patrol. We soon formed a club of sorts, the Extra Fat Left Outs. Anyone was welcome to join, just come sit at the table and order up! We weren't really fat; sometimes it just felt that way. EFLOS are alive and well, even today, as membership is forever. Apologies are in order to the kind citizens of all ages who only wanted a quiet meal at Shoney's. It wasn't happening in the mid-sixties. We ruled the night.

JFK

Most everyone who was alive in 1963 remembers where they were when the news came out that President Kennedy had been assassinated. I was sitting in class at the high school when a very loud voice came over the P. A. System demanding everyone's attention. Our president had been shot. As details were relayed to us, shocked silence gave way to sobbing, and the rest of the day is a blur. Extra security and safety measures kicked in immediately as Oak Ridge was considered a possible target in any emergency situation. The details were secret, but we were aware that the schools, the city, and in fact the whole nuclear reservation had contingency plans for our safety. On that day, all I wanted to do was go home.

The Beatles

That same year, after Christmas, we were caught up in Beatle-Mania. We were still reeling from the assassination of President Kennedy and the Beatles brought us joy. I know exactly where I was the first time I heard "I Want to Hold Your Hand." It was January, 1964. Driving to school with Brenda McClendon, we just passed the water tower at the intersection of Delaware and Outer Drive. The song came on WNOX radio and we were spellbound. When we arrived at the ORHS parking lot, everyone was talking about it. We all listened to the same station on the way to school; with no I-Pods or satellite radio, WNOX was all we had. We couldn't quit talking about this new group from England. The song stayed in my head all day and we could not wait to get back to our cars after school, and happily blast the Beatles all over town.

Applesauce

Today The Secret City hosts rowing regattas on beautiful Melton Hill Lake, attended by university crews from all over the country. But the original Melton Hill regattas were held back in our day. The Clinch River disappeared in Oak Ridge in 1953when the dam was built, creating Melton Hill Lake. The Applesauce League was formed a few years later, for the sole purpose of sponsoring regattas every spring. According to a Teen Talk column written by Jane Crews, one particular race was held at one o'clock on a Sunday afternoon in April, 1963. As of Friday, 21 boats were registered, and more were coming in each day. The dam would be closed, so no currents would affect the race. (Did we actually ask TVA?)

Launching at the Marina, the watercrafts were to be strictly homemade, out of cardboard, wood, and maybe a little Styrofoam, etc., whatever was available. There was actual prize money for the winner and the judges were serious about their task. If anyone tried to sink another boat, they would be disqualified. Judges would be watching from shore and from boats on the water. So beware, anyone touching another boat would be banned from the race. Splashing water was okay. Survivors from sinking boats would be rescued, somehow. Applesauce Regatta fans gathered to give them a hearty welcome from Edgemoor bridge with lots of applesauce, tomatoes, and eggs. As I recall, they were heading for the old Solway bridge. Whether or not any boat ever made it is unknown at this time.

In that same column, Jane reported that I hosted a birthday party for Sandy Shapiro on that same Saturday. After cake and presents, we all rode around in Gage's Great Green Jeep. Hmmm... Wonder where we went?

Shenanigans

I only remember trying alcohol one time. It was close to graduation, and Krattler's older sister Kay bought us a six-pack of Pabst Blue Ribbon Beer. We drove over to Elza Gate, across the railroad tracks, and down into the woods by the water. We opened one can of PBR, passed it around, agreed it was totally yucky, and tossed the rest into the lake! Shameless in our "shenanigans", one night we were out driving around with nothing to do. Sandy wasn't with us. Her family was on vacation. We spotted a wooden commercial "For Sale" sign. Somehow we managed to transport that sign up to East Drive and plant it in the Shapiros' yard, where it remained all week, until they returned from vacation. Needless to say, when they returned from vacation, they got phone calls for weeks from friends, concerned that they were moving, and from strangers, wanting to buy the house. Ted was not happy, and until now, we never 'fessed up.

The Wildcat Band

As in most small southern towns, Friday night football was, and still is, a huge event in Oak Ridge. Sally Armstrong's father was a successful coach, leading us to several state championships, including an undefeated state championship team sophomore year. Jack Armstrong Stadium is named in his honor. The Oak Ridge High School Marching Band was magnificent. Doc Combs demanded perfection, and the band members, especially those inherited from Alice Lyman, gave him nothing less. The cardinal and gray uniforms were state-of-the-art, and our Drum Major, Larry Bender, was spectacular.

He marched with his back nearly parallel to the ground, keeping the band in perfect step, through all the intricate maneuvers. Majorettes, with their sparkling batons, led the show, and halftime was almost as exciting as the game itself. Back then, the band always played the fight song, our Alma Mater, and the National Anthem. The crowd stood, we sang, and we knew the words:

Oak Ridge High, Alma Mater
Stand true in all your might.
Light the way for sons and daughters
With your beacon ever bright.
We will treasure every memory
As we journey down life's way.
We're proud of you and your colors, too.
Here's to you, red and gray!

The Oak Ridge High School Honor creed reads as follows, and we were also expected to know it by heart: "Honor and dignity depend upon the courage and integrity of the individual."

Football

Football for ORHS students didn't always end on Friday nights. Sunday afternoon games were just about as popular. One Sunday in the fall of 1964, two big games were scheduled at the same time. One was between the Gents and Chanticleers and one was between the Penguins and Swank-ettes. The boys were playing at Robertsville Junior High School and the girls at Cedar Hill Elementary. One game ended up being cancelled and the team, out of true team spirit of course, showed up at Cedar Hill to show their support and watch the other teams play. Oh well, the games between the Gents and Chanticleers often ended in a tie, or else no one kept score anyway!

Speaking of the Gents, I have always wondered why "bouncers" were listed in their "official" slate of officers. There must be a story there somewhere...

Drama

Dramatic productions in the Oak Ridge schools were always popular and well-attended, especially at the high school level. I think one reason is that there was money in the budget for props, costumes, and whatever was needed at the time to produce an event that students, faculty, and parents could present with pride. There was also an abundance of volunteers from among the community to help insure success.

The ORHS drama program was directed by English teacher Mr. Bill Lewis. He was a talented, creative, and well-respected task master. He sponsored the Thespians as well as the Masquers Club. I wasn't actively involved in any plays, but I was in the audience every chance I got. One of my favorite productions was "The Chalk Garden," and the production of "The Mouse That Roared," involving over 100 members of the cast and crew, was spectacular. Classmates Tom Spray, Dale Todd, Nancy Leichsenring, and Karol Adam served well as officers in the Masquers Club our senior year. Along with about 50 other drama students, they earned a memorable trip to Atlanta to see "The Sound of Music." They also helped put on a fabulous play at the Oak Ridge Junior Playhouse entitled, "George Washington Slept Here," as a benefit for the Daniel Arthur Rehabilitation Center.

The Christmas Nativity Pageant

Presented by the combined Art, Music and Drama
Departments at Oak Ridge High School, the Christmas
Nativity Pageant was a holiday tradition, first performed in
1943. For the next 22 years, the same four-tableau format,
including all the costumes and sets, were used each season.
There were several performances, during the day and in the
evening, and the school auditorium was always packed.

The music, provided by the full orchestra, mixed chorus,
glee club and choir, varied from year to year. There was no
admission charged; this majestic production was a gift to
the city, and remains in memory, a very special part of our
Oak Ridge heritage. Students and staff worked for weeks,
both during and after school and on weekends, perfecting
every detail.

The pageant opened with a beautiful manger scene on
center stage, and the orchestra played softly as the scribe
began to tell the story of the birth of Jesus. I sang in the
angel chorus, and I will always remember Vicki Hobson's
beautiful solo, "Behold the Star". As her vibrant voice
filled the auditorium, the Angel slowly appeared, high
above the manger scene. As the lights gradually beheld the
large chorus of angels in the sky behind the manger, all the
choral voices rose together in a moving version of "Angels
We Have Heard on High." The Wise Men entered down
the side aisles, crowns and jeweled boxes gleaming by the
light of the Star of Bethlehem, singing "We Three Kings of
Orient Are." The beautiful classical music changed with
each tableau, and familiar carols were beautifully
interwoven.

Every year the finale, Handel's "Hallelujah Chorus" filled the auditorium with beautiful majestic orchestrations as the audience rose to their feet; then the lights dimmed for "Silent Night", and as the audience quietly filed out of the auditorium, you could hear a feather touch the floor. This pageant was a beautiful presentation, and truly it was enjoyed by people of all faiths. I only wish that we, and the current generations, could see the Nativity Pageant again, just one more time.

Graduation

Before we knew it, the spring of 1965 arrived. Thoughts of final exams, college applications, summer plans and graduation filled the air. "Jolly John" Lyell, our popular and talented master of ceremonies, hosted the Senior Banquet, and he stole the show. The soon-to-be-graduated seniors skipped off for a day at Big Ridge while the lowly underclassmen (most of them anyway) stayed at school to study. Scrounge Day found the seniors in ridiculous costumes. Who can ever forget Clifford Busey as the Jolly Green Giant, totally covered in bright green paint, and Pat Gray in her cute little baseball uniform.

It was time to sign annuals, gather up belongings, clean out lockers, and say our good-byes. We tried on our caps and gowns and practiced for graduation, not an easy task for a class of nearly 600 students. Baccalaureate and graduation ceremonies were supposed to be solemn occasions, but mostly I remember the silliness. Someone singing, "My reindeer likes butterrrrrr milk, your reindeer likes…" to the tune of "Pomp and Circumstance," and silly questions like, "If your head is crooked, do you still wear your cap parallel to the floor?" made us laugh.

When graduation finally arrived, I was sad, leaving my friends and this great school which had been my family for all these years: but mainly, heading off to college at the University of North Carolina at Greensboro, I felt confident, prepared, and ready to face whatever this great world would send my way. And I was ready to party!

Big Ridge Week

About 200 girls from all three social clubs were making plans for one final fling, our annual week at Big Ridge, otherwise known as Ranger Robb's Vacation Wonderland. We filled up about 20 cabins or so, and according to our chaperones, who, along with Ranger Robb and his trusty staff, were keeping track of such things, about 100 boys followed us, camping out in tents and cars down behind the horse stables. We enjoyed a wonderful week of swimming, sunning, canoeing, "dream-boating", eating, singing, laughing, loafing, and playing bridge, from early in the morning until not-so-late at night. This was not by choice, but by fear of Ranger Robb's Rule: "All girls in the cabins by 10 and all boys off the porches by 10:30. Ranger check at 10:35, strictly enforced." Besides, Mrs. Shapiro and the other chaperoning moms never went to sleep. It was a wonderful way to end our high school years, and another enchanting memory I will never forget.

Class Reunions

At this point, I would like to offer a special thank you to good friend and classmate, Janice Baker Sanders, for organizing our class reunions through the years and for helping us all to stay in touch through social media. Hopefully this collection of memories will also be helpful in that regard. As I have said, we all have our own tales to tell, and they should be told, but that's another story…

132

134

138

144

147

148

149

Closing Thoughts

Today, Muddy Boots have turned to flip-flops, but the proud determination that inspired our brave parents to build the bomb that saved the world still flows in our veins. We were knitted together, not with threads of DNA, but with threads of USA. Oak Ridge is thriving in a safe nuclear environment. Our prestigious scientific community is home to some of the finest achievements the world has ever known. There are still secrets in The Secret City, many destined never to be told, but life goes on. The heart of our city, the government-built cemesto houses and those in East Village still stand strong. They are among the most well-built, cleverly designed and re-designed houses you could ever imagine. They belong to the engineers, the people who built the Atomic Bomb, and the generations who have chosen to stay here.

Both of our children, Andy and Jennifer, are graduates of the Oak Ridge school system, and today the fourth generation of the Secret City is entering Oak Ridge High School.

Highland View Elementary has become the world famous Children's Museum. Linden is a vibrant elementary school, and Elm Grove has been replaced with a lovely city park. Our beloved Glenwood is officially a Blue Ribbon School, one of the 100 best in the country. Our daughter Jennifer is a secretary at the mammoth Y-12 Nuclear Weapons Facility, continuing the tradition started by her grandfather, some 62 years ago.

Katydids still entertain us with their summer symphonies and the night-blooming cereus, in its original bucket on the patio, continues to amaze us, year after year. And yes, there are many stories, yet to tell. We have come from Mayor Bissell to Mayor Beehan, and the tradition continues, smiles and handshakes all around.

And so, I dedicate these memories…to all Oak Ridgers, past, present, and future, with a challenge to remain honorable stewards of secrets; safe, secure, and steady as we go.

Made in the USA
San Bernardino, CA
28 March 2014